The Sportsman's Library

SALMON FISHING

TOP OF CAST BY MR. JOHN RENNIE, ROD NEARLY VERTICAL.

THE SPORTSMAN'S LIBRARY

SALMON FISHING

BY

W. J. M. MENZIES, F.R.S.E.

Late Inspector of Salmon Fisheries of Scotland
Author of *The Salmon : its life story*
Trout and Sea Trout, etc.

**WITH EIGHT PLATES
AND FIVE FIGURES IN THE TEXT**

ADAM AND CHARLES BLACK
4, 5 & 6 SOHO SQUARE, LONDON, W.1

Australia and New Zealand
THE OXFORD UNIVERSITY PRESS, MELBOURNE

Canada
THE MACMILLAN COMPANY OF CANADA, TORONTO

South Africa
THE OXFORD UNIVERSITY PRESS, CAPE TOWN

India, Pakistan and Burma
MACMILLAN AND COMPANY LIMITED
BOMBAY   CALCUTTA   MADRAS

First Published 1935
Reprinted 1938, and with corrections, 1950

MADE AND PRINTED IN GREAT BRITAIN BY
MORRISON AND GIBB LIMITED, LONDON AND EDINBURGH

CONTENTS

ILLUSTRATIONS

INTRODUCTION

It would be hard for me to mention all those, some now living and some now dead, with whom I have fished, whom I have seen fishing, with whom I have talked fishing, and from whom I have learnt much that is set down here. I cannot refrain from mentioning specially, however, the late Mr. A. H. E. Wood of Glassel who at Cairnton on the Dee worked out the idea of greased line fishing and many other matters in a manner that was, for thoroughness, peculiarly his own. To him and to all of the others my thanks and more than my thanks are due, and to Mr. G. H. Nall also who, with his unfailing kindness, has offered many most helpful criticisms of, and suggestions for, the manuscript.

Thanks are also due to Messrs. J. E. Davis, J. Edwards Moss, P. R. C. Macfarlane, J. E. Young, and John Douglas for the excellent photographs which they have allowed me to use. To Mr. John Rennie I am also indebted for acting as a model for casting, a rôle he is most capable of filling, and to Mr. P. R. C. Macfarlane again for Figures 1 to 3 in the text.

For this present (1950) reprint some minor amendment of, and some more considerable additions to, the original text would be desirable. Printing considerations, however, preclude such alterations at this time.

Chapter I

RODS AND THEIR SELECTION

To the angler of fifty or sixty years ago the selection of a rod for salmon fishing was a comparatively simple matter. If he were a strong man he had one of twenty feet ; if a comparatively puny person eighteen feet had to suffice. In either case he knew the cost before he entered the shop. One shilling per foot was the standard price. It is true he had a choice of woods. Greenheart butts and hickory tops were for a time fashionable ; for a while the top of lancewood in combination with greenheart or hickory or both lower down was all the rage ; at another time washaba was the pick of the connoisseurs. But all these woods, except greenheart, have now entirely gone out of fashion, and to a great extent they have been replaced by split bamboo.

I have handled and fished with more than one of these old rods, and fierce weapons they were. Of one, the proud possession of a ghillie, I have particularly painful recollection. Every inch of twenty feet, it originally possessed either a brass plate at the end or a rubber button of a size in keeping with its length, but of this latter nought remained but what must have been the foundation —a circular brass plate almost the size of the palm of one's hand. Given time in casting, the rod delivered a long and a beautiful line with surprisingly little effort, but in fishing out the cast there was a great deal of weight forward of one's hand. A very few casts taught one that it was better to balance that rod with both one's hands rather than counterbalance the forward weight by pressing that uncompromising brass plate against the softer part of one's anatomy !

Like some of the old golf shafts and wooden heads, the timber of many of these rods was excellent. In some the grain was short, and an acute break might result ; in others the wood was soft, and bends, either of temporary or permanent shape, quickly developed. A very well-known Scottish angler of the time who died in the early years of this century had a thorough, if somewhat rough, method of testing the merits of a new rod. He was a man several inches over six feet in height, strong in proportion, and he proceeded after letting out as much line as he could wield on the lawn, to lash the rod horizontally from side to side. If it broke under this trial it was considered bad and returned to the maker ; if it remained straight, then it was at least worth further test at the river and was retained !

Fortunately for us modern and weaker mortals the days of the terrifyingly long rods have gone. And with them, unfortunately for our pockets, has gone also the satisfying cheapness. Fortunately also for our peace of mind the varying combinations of wood are likewise a thing of the past.

Nowadays only two materials are employed for rod-making, and these are either greenheart or split bamboo. The former may be had with joints of the conventional socket form, or the union between the different parts may be effected by means of a splice whipped together with an outer binding. In the case of split bamboo rods, the longitudinal pieces are glued together to form a hexagonal final section, and they may be either single or double built, both being either with or without a steel centre : the joints for these rods are invariably of the socket type although in the case of smaller rods for trout or sea trout one-piece weapons may be obtained.

The prevailing fashion to-day is undoubtedly for

split bamboo, or as they are generally termed, split cane rods. They are necessarily more expensive than greenheart rods, and price is only too often a criterion of quality and value—and therefore of usefulness. Those in a position to know also assure me that the supply of really good greenheart has become more and more restricted, whereas an ample quantity of bamboo always exists, from which a selection of sufficient quantity of the best class can be made. Owing to the fashion and prevalent demand, it would also seem that the number of workmen competent to deal with greenheart and to turn out really first-class rods is now very limited. Consequently in most of the rod-maker's shops and the shops of those who sell rods produced by the larger factories, one will now find an infinitely larger selection among split bamboo than among greenheart rods. Not only will the range in lengths probably be greater, but the variations in weight and action at each length will also be larger. The proportion of really good to bad rods may, however, be rather lower, for it by no means follows that a split bamboo rod is necessarily a good rod. The workmanship and finish, it is true, may be beyond reproach, but the action and fishing efficiency may be indifferent, although no doubt the salesman who will try to sell one such a rod, as I know by experience, will appear to be exceedingly pained if one tells him so.

Personally I have to admit to a predilection for a greenheart rod of the spliced variety for salmon fishing, although I own and habitually use others made of bamboo. A spliced greenheart seems to me to feel more of a unit, more closely approaching the ideal of a one-piece rod than a rod of either greenheart with socket joints or split bamboo. A spliced greenheart made and balanced for the purpose is the only rod which is really adapted for switching or the so-called Spey cast. They are not everybody's rods, however. They appear to be old-fashioned. They are slightly more trouble to put up than the other type, and to some people the splices appear to be clumsy. In the smaller sizes greenheart tops are perhaps more liable to fracture than are those of split bamboo.

I have even known ghillies who did not know how to make the splice properly. This may be done with either leather thongs or sticking tape sold for the purpose. In either case the two parts are held together and a start made at the top by taking a turn of the tape over itself, or three turns of the leather thong over the end which has been laid back down the rod. The tape is then continued with even turns and finished off again by one turn over itself at the other end. The thong, after the three closely set turns, is continued down the splice with wider spacing, and then finished off with three close turns and two half-hitches at the end of the splice : finally, the end of the leather may be tied down, to be out of the way if desired, by a single turn of fine twine or sticking tape.

An angler who will put prejudice out of his mind and who will give a really good spliced greenheart rod a fair trial will, I venture to think, be undeniably attracted by its feel and its uniform action throughout. This type of rod is not to be found to perfection in all the shops even of those who make a show of stocking greenheart rods. It is the speciality of comparatively few firms, and it is to one of these that the prospective purchaser should turn, and to whom more than possibly he will apply after trying such a rod belonging to friend or companion.

Failing a spliced greenheart rod from a special establishment, the average angler will find a better selection of split bamboo than of greenheart rods in the shops where he is likely to deal and, provided cost is not a matter of great moment, and care and time are taken in making a selection, he is more likely to get a really good rod of the former material.

First-class split bamboo rods are, however, undeniably expensive, and should they be rather beyond the capacity of the purse it would probably be wise to extend the search for a greenheart which can be obtained at about half the cost. Sometimes it is also possible to obtain a thoroughly good second-hand rod either at a sale of tackle by auction or other means ; but in this case, as in the case of all articles bought by the same channels, special caution has to be exercised lest one is let in for a bad bargain. A rod normally lasts a long time and may throughout its life be either a pleasure or the very reverse to use. It therefore pays not only to get the very best quality that one can afford, but also to take some trouble in choosing one which is inherently good and which is the most suitable for both the angler and the purpose to which it is normally to be put.

If a novice is about to commence a store of implements, for one rod almost invariably leads to the possession of others, my strong advice to him is either to take an angling friend to the tackle-makers or, after explaining his approximate requirements, to have a selection of say three rods of the appropriate type sent out to be tested, if possible at the waterside, by some experienced fishing acquaintance. As I have said above, all rods, even well-made rods, are by no means first-class for throwing a line, and a salesman with the best will and greatest honesty in the world towards the angler has to get rid of all his stock, some perhaps rather in the hope that they may suit the particular style of the angler to whom they go.

In choosing a greenheart rod the ' grain ' (that is, the darker parts which have the appearance of lines in the wood) should be examined. If the grain is short, the rod should on no account be taken, as a break is very likely to occur following a minimum of unusual strain. This is particularly the case with a rod with socket joints, in which the break is usually just at the end of either ferrule. In a bamboo rod this particular fault is not to be found, but it should be examined to see that no portion of the bamboo has been overburnt in the course of preparation, and that all the whippings, especially round the base of the ferrules, have been properly finished. In the rods of both materials the ferrules should also be looked at to see that they are a close and exact fit. The old-fashioned method of tying two joints together by a loop of string round a projecting fastener on each has now been entirely superseded by one or other locking device, but with some of these the male part of the ferrule is apt to rotate slightly after use during a long day if the whole joint is not an exact and moderately tight fit.

In the case of a fly rod the top should be specially tried to ensure that it is satisfactory. After flexion it should spring back to its original straightness smartly. If there be any feeling of dullness in the action, or if the recovery to a straight line be not absolutely complete, then attention should be directed towards another rod.

Whether a steel-centred rod be bought is a matter of personal choice. The steel centre is not likely to make a great deal of difference one way or the other, although some people hold that it is a disadvantage.

No greater mistake is possible than making the final choice of a rod in a shop where it can only be waved about gently in a limited area, and where it is quite impossible to try it out by casting a suitable line of reasonable length. After deciding on the particular type and action desired a preliminary selection can well be made within the confined space ; but before the ultimate purchase is irrevocably settled (so important is this point, that I repeat what I said above), two or three of the most promising should be taken at least on to grass, and tried out with reel and line by someone competent to cast sufficiently well for the purpose.

Apart from inherent defects of material or

J. E. Davis.

START OF FORWARD THROW BY MR. JOHN RENNIE

workmanship, probably the worst fault which a salmon rod can possess is a middle joint which is weak in comparison with the top and the butt to which it is mated. It is moreover a fault which is by no means uncommon. It may extend to the whole of the joint or to a particular spot, which in many cases will be found to be about two-thirds of the way up the joint. On the other hand, this joint should not be unusually heavy or stiff in comparison with the other two ; it should harmonize with them throughout its whole length. Nor should the butt be overstiff. The action must extend right down to the button.

There must be no suspicion of knuckling or hinging anywhere in the rod, for if it exists it spoils not only the feel but also the casting power. When moved vigorously up and down so that the spring of the whole rod from button to tip is brought out, this defect, if it exists, usually becomes apparent even in the shop trial, although if confined to one spot it may not be found until a line is brought into action. In general ' feel ' a rod should be light and responsive, in proportion to its length and power, and the quicker the rebound when in motion the better.

A disadvantage to which many British rods are prone, although those built in America in this respect are often better, is that the point of balance is too far forward. This is particularly so I think in the case of rods of twelve feet and of the lighter fourteen feet lengths. Modern rods are so comparatively light that the total weight of the timber and fittings in them is not of great moment, but whether the point of balance is close to the angler's hands or is far forward up the butt does make a very considerable difference. In the former case he has little but the total weight of the rod to hold up, but in the latter his forward hand forms a fulcrum on which considerable strain has to be brought to balance the long ' overhang ' of weight.

A little experiment in ascertaining the exact point of balance and in using the rod with the hands farther up the butt than usual will soon demonstrate the cogency of this point. When a rod is balanced with a suitable reel complete with line, a rough guide can be obtained during the shop trial and, other things being equal, the rod having the point of balance nearest to the reel should be chosen.

Unless one is very lucky it will probably be impossible to get any rod which is ideal in this respect, but sometimes an improvement can be effected by having the reel fittings (if they be not of the free moving, self-locking type) moved slightly backwards without destroying the convenience or comfort for one's hands. In the shorter and lighter rods some good may also be done by increasing the size and weight of the button. In fact, one very well-known angler went so far as to have brass buttons (with rubber end pads) of various weights made for use with some of his rods and for the purpose of testing the many which were sent to him. Good balance, however, should on no account be obtained by a light, weak, ' sloppy ' top.

A ' top heavy ' rod or one in which the action does not take place evenly right from the tip down to below one's hands in the butt is, as I have said, one to be avoided. But to this there is one exception, and that is in the case of a rod intended primarily for switching, or for use where the Spey cast will often be employed. In this case the necessary action is rather different. The rod should be to some extent dominated by the top joint, which should be heavier than is normally the case. This will impart to the upper part of the middle joint a feeling of movement which in other cases is so much to be avoided ; but in this instance the movement results from the somewhat excessive strength of the top rather than from any undue weakness in any part of the middle joint.

The same general considerations hold for spinning

rods as for fly rods except that it is even more impossible to test them properly without a full-scale trial. The stiffness required to deal with the weight of lead and bait is such that the action can be properly brought out and any weaknesses exposed only when the rod is actually dealing with that for which it is designed or intended.

Agate butt and end rings are now fitted as standard on practically all fly rods, and no criticism of their use is possible provided they are of adequate size, and properly protected against injury by knocks or falls. On fly rods especially, the end ring is often too small to give the line, and particularly the thicker part of a tapered line, as free run as would be the case were the ring larger. Do not, however, be tempted to fit agate rings throughout a fly rod on account of their smooth and comparatively friction-less appearance. Their aggregate weight is such as to spoil entirely the feel and balance of the rod.

Until late in the last century the intermediate rings were of the loose, circular, hang-down variety which swayed backwards and forwards with the run of the line, and which must have allowed a minimum of free run for shooting line during a cast. The advent of upright and then snake rings was heralded as a great improvement, as no doubt it was, though these in turn have now given place to bridge rings on the products of the majority of rod-makers. The reason for this last change I could never understand. In theory I suppose it was to protect the rod from wear by the line, signs of which, however, seem never to be present. Except for this mythical benefit I could never see any advantage in this so-called improvement, and to my mind snake rings are still decidedly preferable. Bridge rings are more liable to get knocked out of shape than snake rings. The wire for bridge rings is sometimes of angular rather than round section. On almost all rods they are far too small, so that the frictional resistance is increased both by the shape

2

of the wire and the fact that the line has only a restricted space for free movement. Snake rings of ample size for each length of rod are light, being of the minimum possible length of wire, offer little frictional resistance, and give a clear space for the free run of the line between the ring and the rod which is as large as is possible. The change from bridge to snake rings can easily be effected, or they may be specially indicated for a rod which is to be constructed. Perhaps one reason for the small bridge rings is that they look neat and tidy.

A few words on the care of a rod may not be out of place.

The ferrules of a rod of that type should be very lightly but evenly oiled or greased so that the bronze does not degenerate on the surface. Vaseline is said to be bad, why, is not very clear, and certainly in use it does not appear to be harmful, but any kind of animal fat, or a very thin, clear oil in the smallest possible quantity may be used. In putting up or taking down the rod the two ferrules alone should be grasped and turned. The firm grasp by the wood and the equally firm twist given so often by a ghillie is obviously one of the best possible ways of shaking the well-made and proper joint between wood and metal. If the joint is excessively tight when being taken down, the aid of a second person, one to hold each part, is of great assistance. If it still refuses to yield, the application of gentle heat, *e.g.* from a candle, to expand the female part, may also help. But any such difficulty should be regarded as a sign of lack of attention.

The stoppers for the ferrules are often a source of annoyance. When not in use they have an unpleasant habit of being lost. A bit of tape sewn down on the inside of the flap of the rod case so as to form two loops, each of which exactly fits one of the stoppers, forms a safe and convenient repository for them.

When fishing at one place for a period it is often

convenient not to take down rod and reel each day. Pegs for the purpose of holding the rod horizontal are often provided, but unless closely spaced they are not satisfactory as a curve in the rod may develop in one or more places. A whole wood shelf, just wide enough to hold rod and reel, is much more satisfactory. The line may then be led through a ring placed on the end of the shelf to a large wooden open reel, on an axis fastened to the wall, which will act as a line drier. If this practice be adopted, the reel should be taken off and cleaned and oiled at least once a week.

On that essential fitting for a rod, the reel, one cannot go far wrong. For each length of rod a certain size is indicated, though a choice of say a quarter of an inch in overall measurement is quite possible. Due regard should be paid, as I said before, to balancing the rod, and in the smaller sizes one of the contracted drum type which is larger but narrower than the normal is a material help in reeling in. The round line guard, whether of agate or hardened steel, through which the line is led to the first rod ring, I do not like as it seems to help the line to pile up in the centre of the reel instead of assisting an even spread.

Reels differ greatly in quality, and in this case the most expensive is almost always the best. The bearings of a reel have to do a lot of work and are sometimes subject to rather rough treatment, so that they have to be good. The cheaper reels are not only of inferior finish, which is perhaps a matter of no great moment, but both the bearings and the check mechanism may wear very quickly. Some may be satisfactory but many are quite the reverse. If the question of price be very important, it is far better to get a part-worn reel of first-class make rather than a new reel of inferior workmanship. A good reel should always be well looked after, taken to pieces, and thoroughly cleaned and oiled whenever necessary.

Chapter II

LINES AND CASTS

Parallel with the improvement in the materials for, and construction of, rods has occurred a development in the types and manufacture of lines. Many of the older fashion of lines still exist not only on reels of historical interest in museums and private houses but also in odd corners of some anglers' establishments. On examination, these will be found to be of twisted horsehair varying in thickness according to the purpose for which they were intended. They are to a great degree waterproof and are somewhat stiff, but when tapered into, and continued by, a horsehair cast they must have been very sweet lines to use with the rods and methods of casting then extant. To our present-day ideas and for modern rods they are far too light for anything other than fishing with a very short line from a boat for trout. In any case it is perhaps as well that they are out of date, for with the rise of motor transport the supply of the necessary raw material must have inevitably become smaller and smaller. Nowadays the hairs of the tail of a grey mare, the desideratum of connoisseurs, must be a very scarce commodity. Human hair from Japan used for lines as late as about 1900 is also probably rather difficult to secure.

After hair lines those constructed of silk of square plait gradually developed. What exactly may have been the course of events I do not know, but comparatively rapidly silk lines dressed with linseed oil, dried and hardened, came into general use. They were of the same diameter throughout their distance and could be purchased up to a reasonable length in one piece. They carried a minimum of dressing, they were distinctly hard, and had the merit of not becoming sticky or tacky except under extreme provocation. Such was the comparative lightness of these lines that anglers at first filled their reels entirely with them. Soon, however, the advantages of the use of heavier lines began to be apparent, and their disadvantages from the aspects of both casting and fishing and the size of reel necessary to accommodate the required length were also realized. No man can hope to cast one hundred or more yards of line when fly-fishing, and the surplus beyond the fishing length was replaced with a subsidiary line, spliced on to the casting line, of undressed silk, flax, or hemp of equal strength but very much smaller diameter. The disabilities of the level heavy line were removed by having the required weight only for the greater part of the line and a portion at one or each end gradually tapering off to the desired state of fineness at the point where it joins the cast. The late Mr. G. M. Kelson invented the first tapered line and it was made, I believe, by Messrs. Morris Carsewell & Co.

Now practically all lines used in fly-fishing are of the oil-dressed silk type double tapered (*i.e.* with a tapering portion at each end), forty-two yards in length, and the vast majority of anglers use silk backing of a strength commensurate with that of the line. Together line and backing should comfortably fill the reel ; to be overfull results in the line being pinched and cut between the revolving drum and the frame, and if it be not full enough some rapidity in the recovery of line is lost.

A total length (line and backing) of a hundred or a hundred and twenty yards will suffice for the ordinary rivers of Great Britain, although if one be fishing where large fish are normally expected, the water is unusually wide, or to follow a hooked fish is difficult, greater length may on a few occasions be desirable.

The modern line, like so much of the rest of our fishing gear, is an excellent production, but it has one failing. Many lines are only too liable to become sticky or tacky in spite of all precautions which the angler may take in the form of removing the line from the reel and drying it carefully after fishing, or hanging it up in loose coils when not in use. It is a fault to which the earlier lines were not nearly so prone, and it is one which is difficult to guard against when selecting a new line.

Lines are now made with two types of finish, one bearing a highly polished surface (this type often being a dark-green colour) and the other a dull oily-looking surface with usually a basic brown coloration. I may have been fortunate with the brown oily lines, but in my experience they appear to be less liable to become sticky than the polished green variety. Some of the brown are certainly less heavily loaded with oil than are the green, and therefore are lighter at corresponding diameters. A third type of line is of a somewhat lighter green shade speckled with black, and so far as I am aware this was one of the earliest patterns made. At first it seems to have been known as the American or Canadian line. This type still usually has a harder dressing which is less liable to become sticky than the others, but its drawback is that before it is worn out it becomes weak in places and will ultimately break up into a series of pieces, each only a few inches or a foot or two long. While sound, however, these lines are pleasant and efficient in use.

A partial cure of a sticky line may be effected by immersing it in a suspension of whiting powder, or one of the special preparations sold for the purpose, for a time and then drying and carefully re-polishing.

In choosing a line comparatively little care is now required, such is the general level of their excellence. One can only see that they carry no suspicion of even the beginning of stickiness, and that the surface is well finished with no sign of manufacturing defects. It is perhaps better to obtain any lines one requires from the larger town dealers who are likely to carry comparatively new stock, rather than from somewhat remote shops where lines may have been held in far from ideal conditions for some time.

The matter of the selection of the size of line for a particular rod is more difficult, and of considerably more importance than the effort to pick the best of those all of which are of almost uniform high quality. If the choice be left to the tackle-maker, one will almost always carry off a line too light for the purpose intended, so much so that it may no more than fit a rod two feet shorter than that for which it was bought. A line should be heavy enough to bring the whole power and feel of the rod from top to button into play when a line of ordinary fishing length is in use. Only in this way can the maximum power of the rod be exercised with the minimum of effort by the fisherman. If the line be too light so that only the top or the top and the upper part of the middle joint is made to 'work,' casting, especially against or across the wind, can never be satisfactory, and an undue amount of energy will be used up in the process —a form of 'tennis elbow' may even result. If error be made, it is better that one err on the side of having a line that is too heavy : this may be a little hard on the rod, but the results will be infinitely better, and to some extent the extra weight may be compensated by having a shorter line in the air, and 'shooting' more from the hand. In any event, the line should be heavy enough actually to pull out the length waiting to be shot.

It is easier to give a warning against the purchase of a line that is too light than to suggest what is the correct size for any particular length of rod. Lines are usually sold by numbers, and for each number a certain length of rod is nominated. The loose designations are common to many other articles of fishing tackle. It would be better were lines marked with the wire gauge measurement of the main part and at the extreme ends together with the length of taper and the total weight.

A wet line should be run on to a line drier or hung up in loose coils. Drying by the latter method is perhaps the more certain, and is not fraught with great danger of entanglement if in pulling the line off the reel the loops are kept small and in orderly array in the hand : when all the dressed line is off, a length of the backing can be pulled free and tied into a loop in which the coils of dressed line can hang free. If any doubt be felt as to the line running free when replacing it on the reel, the coils should be held in the hand in the same manner as when running off the reel, and starting from the backing end (*i.e.* the direct reverse of the way in which it was laid into the hand) it should be carefully laid back, coil by coil, into large free loops on the floor. Failing this method or a proper line drier (which may be purchased at a wide variety of prices), a line may be run off on to the back of a chair or on another convenient article of furniture —provided it be one's own or the owner thereof has no objections to the practice !

The cast of gut or the newer nylon is or should be a direct continuation of the line. Casts are to be had in a much greater range of sizes than lines, and normally I think the average tackle-maker and many anglers are apt to fall into error opposite to that which I have stressed above, and to choose casts which are too thick, or at least thicker than is desirable or necessary for the purpose intended. For early spring fishing with big flies of size 4/0 and upwards a thick cast is of course necessary, and in this case one and a half yards of treble-twisted gut, slightly tapered, followed by

J. E. Davis.

FINISH OF CAST BY MR. JOHN RENNIE.
Note position of rod and hands for cut into wind.

one and a half yards of heavy single gut will be both useful and economical. For very large flies 6/o¼ and upwards, the heaviest gut is undoubtedly an advantage, but it is extremely expensive, and unless one's purse be long something less costly will suffice. As a matter of fact nylon is a very effective substitute for gut and very much cheaper in price. It can be obtained in any length and the consequential paucity of knots as well as lack of glitter form distinct advantages. Though knots be few they must however be properly made for, in nylon, they are the weakness. The blood knot must be used throughout (see page 69) and the turle knot is the safest for joining fly to cast.

When the flies are much below 4/0 size, however, a piece of treble is not necessary either for mechanical or financial reasons, and a cast of single gut nine feet or so in length is adequate for nearly all occasions.

A tapered cast helps casting and often fishing also in the smaller sizes. With the larger sizes of fly it is not so necessary as the difference in size of cast and the end of the line is not great. When medium and the smaller sizes of fly are in use, however, a taper is most desirable. In the latter cases it is probable that the line will be a great deal thicker than a cast suitable for the fly and the fishing conditions, and some gradual diminution of the difference will be required.

A help in the merging of line to cast in the case of the smaller sizes may be provided by splicing a link, consisting of one or at the most two lengths of very fine triple gut, with a loop at the end, on to the reel line. The cast is then made fast by putting its loop over the other loop and passing the remainder of the cast starting from the free end through the loop of the spliced-on length. Care should be taken also to taper the splice properly by having the component parts of the triple gut of unequal length, for if they terminate at the same point on the line, danger exists of hinging and of a fracture occurring there.

The larger tackle-makers now stock both tapered and level casts, and it should be possible to make a choice from their stock of any cast desired, or they will make up casts to any specification.

If one has time to spare, however, it adds much to the interest of fishing and ensures that one has exactly what one thinks is best, if one makes up casts as required throughout the season. It is then possible to vary the taper, the length, or the strength of casts from day to day as water or weather conditions alter, and the sizes of the flies in use are changed. Certain firms specialize in dealing in gut. It may be obtained in hanks of one hundred strands each, either raw as it comes from Spain, not picked over and unstained, or in the same condition but stained. In either event it is roughly graded into sizes and lengths, but a certain latitude of selection as to uniformity of size, length, and quality is inevitable in this gut from the wholesale market. Trimmed gut, stained, of more even length, size, and quality may also be obtained. Gut is sold in lengths of from ten to sixteen inches, and the different sizes are dealt in under the original Spanish trade descriptions of *fina* (the thinnest for salmon, though *refina* and *refinucha* are two further trout sizes) to *Royal hebra* (the thickest), but the actual sizes in the various roughly graded hanks naturally overlap considerably so that only a selection (together with some $\frac{1}{4}$ and $\frac{1}{2}$ drawn) is necessary to give all the sizes required. Properly cared for, stored in an air- and light-tight container in a cool, dry place (as described in Chapter XV) and never wetted, such gut should keep in perfect order for many seasons.

If economy of expenditure be urgently necessary, then a selection of gut substitute in coils of various sizes will also give all the supply required, but the softness of this material in the lighter sizes with a full length cast is apt to be a drawback.

Casts may be stained in various colours, but in practice only blue, green, and brown are common. The first-named used to be the most popular but generally was, and when used still often is, somewhat fugitive after being some time in water. Some casts are of a most attractive pale, dull green (which also fades to some extent), which seems to me to combine as far as possible invisibility to the fish with a sense of effectiveness to the fisherman. Attempts have been made from time to time to break up the line of the cast in the water by employing several colours in sections throughout its length, although it is difficult to show any definite improvement in the catch from this effect.

The one departure from what one might call the standard method of colouring casts with various dyes is that in which silver is deposited in the gut and used as the colouring medium either through a solution directly coloured by light, or one in which a light sensitive salt is exposed and subsequently developed in the photographic manner. This process undoubtedly is excellent. It gives a very pleasing colour for use in peat and other water, provides a surface with diminished flash or glint, and in my experience seems undoubtedly to delay to a marked extent the fraying of the gut when in use. The difficulty is to stop entirely the action of the salt at the desired point. It is apt to continue until the cast in use becomes too opaque, and in my opinion the casts sold after treatment by a patented process of this kind are much too dark. The advantages of the transparent and invisible qualities of gut are largely lost if the dyeing process converts its appearance almost to that of a dull copper wire. Otherwise I think there can be no two opinions as to its merits.

Chapter III

FLY-FISHING : CASTING

There are those who affect to despise any form of salmon angling other than that with an artificial fly. With them I have to confess a certain amount of sympathy, although I have also to admit that a judicious mixture of all methods will almost certainly lead to the largest total bag in the course of the season.

Certainly fly-fishing is one of the oldest of all the angling arts, and fly-fishing for salmon probably descended from similar fishing for trout. In fact, almost all the earlier angling writers, and some even to a comparatively late date, who refer to the subject, deprecate in more or less strong terms any attempt to take a salmon owing to its great strength and vigour, and the extreme unlikelihood of bringing it to the bank. We must suppose that up to very recent times the same sort of idea has persisted, indeed still persists, among some anglers and tackle-makers, since gear for salmon fishing has been regarded as of necessity strong and cumbersome. Thick casts and cart-rope-like lines seem to have been regarded as essential and it is small wonder that angling for salmon was held to be almost useless except in porter-coloured floods and high water.

It is rather curious that this old belief should have arisen and persisted, and that few should have tested whether such strength of tackle was really necessary. The pressure which even a big rod is able to exert is surprisingly small, as may readily be seen if one attempts to lift, not swing, a half pound trout directly out of the water. It is unlikely that the old, long, rather whippy rods would pull more than the shorter, stiffer, and stronger modern weapons. Some of my own belonging to the latter category I have put to the test of pulling on a spring balance with a force as great as would ever be used in practical fishing without subjecting the tackle to an absolute breaking strain. The results achieved with ten yards of line out are as follows :

Rod	Pounds Pulled
Stout 16 ft. Split bamboo . . .	6 to 8
Very Stout 14 ft. Greenheart . .	$4\frac{1}{2}$ to 6
Medium 14 ft. Greenheart . . .	4 to 5
Medium 12 ft. Split bamboo . .	$3\frac{1}{2}$ to $4\frac{1}{2}$
Light 11 ft. 6 in. Split bamboo . .	$2\frac{1}{2}$ to 3

These figures effectively dispose of the necessity for tackle of great strength, although heavy lines are needed for casting, and strong casts may be required to take the strain of large flies and the jolt necessary to drive such hooks home.

The action necessary for overhead casting has changed in recent years with the change of rod type, just as the sweeping swing which suited the long supple shafts, and somewhat ungainly heads of the old-fashioned golf clubs has been altered to the shorter swing and more direct blow which is fitted to the modern stiffer clubs.

If the beginner in salmon angling has no knowledge of trout fishing and is situated within reach of one or other of the casting schools which are now in existence, I would strongly recommend that he or she start by taking a few lessons from the expert in charge. In so doing more of the rudiments of the art will be acquired than is possible from the printed page and, most important of all, the foundation of a good style will be laid. The acquisition of the last attribute, on which accuracy, lightness, and distance depend, can also be encouraged by watching good fishermen by the waterside or at a casting tournament.

For the first practical trial a stretch of water should be selected with a low, unencumbered bank and a moderate current. If, however, no 'schooling' has been done, possibly some absolutely still water may for the first time or two be even easier, since the line is picked up and cast forward in practically the same direction, and no turn in the air is necessary to alter its course from parallel with the bank at the end of the cast to across the stream at the commencement of the new one.

Having, with the aid of a friend learned in these matters, selected a rod suitable for one's person and one's purse and a line well adapted for the instrument, one should attach a cast and fly of medium weight and size. A few yards of line are now flicked out as best one may until the 'feel' of the rod is brought out, and one is able to realize what the whole thing is meant to do. The earlier attempts, whether made in running or still water, will also be found to be easier if the line is greased, since one of the chief difficulties of the beginner is to bring the line to the surface before the cast is made. Owing to inevitable slowness it sinks considerably deeper than may later be the case.

We will suppose that we are standing on the left bank of a river or facing some still water in a position where we may cast over our right shoulder without fear of catching fences, trees, or bushes ; to begin with the grass of the bank will prove to be quite effective enough in catching the fly. If stones replace grass it is better to resign oneself to fishing for a considerable part of the time with a hook without a point ! The first attempts, and some for a long time afterwards, will inevitably be much too even and gentle. The rod, properly grasped with right hand towards the top of the cork grip and the left between reel and button, will be waved to and fro with the point well down behind and in front. Later the backward swing may be similar but shorter, and the forward throw after the manner of using a whip—as an unkind critic once remarked ' like a peasant thrashing a donkey.' Slowly it will be realized that casting in this manner has its very strict limitations, and that an expensive rod, reel, and line are hardly necessary for its exploitation.

The first thing that has to be learnt about serious casting is that the line, except for that portion which is shot from the hand (of which more anon), must be extended in the air as far behind as in front of the angler. To do this a sharp flick must be given to the upward lift of the rod as the line is retrieved from the water. But first of all, if any material length of line is out, a preliminary pull must be made by raising the rod point so as partially to release the line (if it is not greased) from the depths of the water in which it is buried. The point may then be sharply lowered, the slack recovered through the rings by hand, and the cast proper commenced. The cast is made by raising both hands, but chiefly the right, the left acting principally as a fulcrum, so that the line is thrown sharply into the air and behind the angler. On no account should the rod be allowed to follow the same course : it must be definitely checked when it is vertical, and thereafter permitted to travel only a very short distance beyond this point ; then a definite pause should be made while the line has time to travel the much longer course which it necessarily has to pursue.

The finest caster I have ever seen followed with his eyes the flight of line and fly backwards until the moment arrived for the forward movement. This is a counsel of perfection which probably will not be copied by fishermen in ordinary circumstances. Normally one waits until one feels the pull of the straight line. The forward movement of the rod is then begun, and it must be as decisive and definite as the upward flick and the backward throw. The precise moment for stopping the backward drive, the length of pause, and the moment for starting the forward thrust is known as timing, and on it depends the whole success of the cast. If the backward movement be carried too far, or the wait for the extension of the line be over-delayed, the fly will fall and catch in any obtrusive object. At the best the forward cast will be in-different, if not a complete failure. If on the other hand the forward movement be made too soon or the point be brought down too violently, the line will reach the water in a heap not far from the rod point, or peradventure will end in a poor result far short of the maximum distance with splashing and loops of line on the water.

Timing is most important, and I do not hesitate to stress the point by reiteration. Until it has been acquired, the budding angler should be con-tent to keep to the use of quite a short line, and if he masters this his time will have been well spent.

Once he is able to keep in control a moderate length of line he should not be content until he can place it where he wishes with lightness, pre-cision, and absolute straightness. Not that I mean to say this is absolutely necessary for successful fishing. Far from it. Many a good fish has been caught by a bad cast. I have seen a grilse come up and pick a fly out of numerous coils of cast, but if full advantage of all available water is to be obtained by long and accurate casting this careful preliminary groundwork is absolutely essen-tial. The downstream foot, that is the left foot when on the left bank (looking downstream), should always be extended slightly in front of the other as an aid to balance.

We will now presume that the angler has had sufficient preliminary instruction and practice to be able to hold the rod and to cast a short line, and that he is standing, still on the left bank of the river with the length of line which he can

J. Edwards Moss.

CASTING OVER 'WRONG' SHOULDER.
THE FORWARD THROW BY JOHN GEORGE EDWARDS.

J. Edwards Moss.

CASTING OVER THE 'WRONG' SHOULDER.
BY JOHN GEORGE EDWARDS.

manage extended below him in the stream. The old-fashioned ghillie's advice to him would then be to cast at an angle of 45 degrees across and downstream with everything between reel and fly dead taut. For purposes of learning this is no bad instruction.

The first difficulty additional to that of pure casting, however, now arises. The line has to be retrieved from one direction and delivered in another. This may be achieved by two methods. The first and simplest is to lift the line rather behind the angler by inclining the rod in that direction during the course of its travel from the horizontal to, and a little beyond, the vertical. After the line is fully extended, the direction of aim is changed to the desired point, the rod is brought forward and downward in that plane, and the line naturally follows. In the second method, which is of particular use when one is wading, the line is passed on its upward track in front of the angler by means of what a cricketer would call the beginning of a round-arm cast, and is then brought forward by passing the rod point and upper (that is in this case the right) hand through the greater part of an ellipse until the hand is returned to its normal position in front of the angler and the rod is again horizontal.

This description of the overhead cast in its two forms is necessarily very general in its terms since once the principle has been grasped, each angler will be able to work out the details for himself. The three essentials are a firm but not tight grip of the rod, the upward flick which will pass the line backwards to its full extent, and the timing for the forward throw.

As the angler progresses in practice and experience, he will be able to deal with more and more line until finally he finds he has reached a stage at which the rod will comfortably lift no greater length. He may then draw off from the

reel another couple of yards and allow this to hang
down in a loop, at the same time holding the line
leading from the bottom ring tight against the rod
by the right (*i.e.* the upper) hand. If he be casting
properly, a distinct pull will be felt on the line in
his hand after the rod has arrived at the end of
the forward throw and when the line is almost
fully extended, but before it has reached the water.
If the slack in the loop be then released it will run
out, and the length of the cast will be increased by
this amount. This is called ' shooting ' line, and
is a device by means of which the cast may be
lengthened by as much as ten yards or so. If a
line of a weight to suit the rod be properly cast
it will literally tear out of the angler's hand by its
own weight and impetus the line waiting to be
' shot.' If the cast be well made and this pull
be not felt, it is practically certain that the line
is too light. In fact, say with a cast of fifteen or
twenty yards and only two or three yards shot the
pull should be sufficient to move the check of the reel
through two or three cogs after the shot line has
sped through the rings. When one is wading, or if
any considerable quantity of line is to be shot,
it is held in a series of small loops in the hand.
I have also seen some anglers divide the excess
line between the two hands.

Two methods of delivering the cast are possible.
In the one, the line is fully extended in the air
a short distance above the water, the fly alights
first and the line then falls lightly, in comparison
with its weight, upon the surface. To achieve this
the angler has to aim rather above the surface,
and should not bring his rod point below a certain
fixed level which can only be ascertained by experience and trial and error.

In the other method the rod point is brought
down considerably nearer the water. The line first
strikes the surface close to the rod point and then
runs out, as if it were being uncoiled, until the

fly alights last of all. This last looks very neat
and effective, the line goes out absolutely straight
and is comparatively little affected by a head or
side wind. When carried out by an expert with
care, it creates practically no greater disturbance
on the surface of the stream than does a line cast
in the other manner, but when executed by the
careless or non-expert it certainly creates a good
deal of unnecessary movement, expecially in calm
and rather still water. In some cases the line is
literally thrashed down with complete disregard
of the effect which it may have on all the fish in
the neighbourhood.

When casting from the other (that is the right)
bank, the position of the hands on the rod is
reversed, and the left becomes the top hand. The
right foot is also advanced. A flat, calm day is not
ideal for fishing, but is certainly a material help
to the beginner when casting. At that time any
kind of wind of any strength is a hindrance, but
later various ' airts o' wind,' as the Scots ghillie
has it, will be found to react in very different
manner on the fisherman. For casting, perhaps
the greatest help is that which blows gently from
behind past the angler's upstream ear—the greatest
hindrance certainly comes from the wind which
blows across and upstream right into the angler's
face. The favourable wind, if too strong, may
become a curse if it blows the line down so that in
passing outwards it strikes the angler's clothing,
or an actual danger if, as may easily be the case,
it results in a large hook affixing itself to his person.
An unfavourable wind may on occasions make
angling at the best a labour, and at the worst
practically impossible.

When the ought-to-be favourable wind becomes
too strong, it may be dodged by changing hands
on the rod and casting over the downstream
shoulder. This keeps fly and line quite clear of
the angler, and if difficulty be felt in doing the

complete change of direction motions in one movement, under these circumstances they may be accomplished in two parts by first making a false cast with a short line, and then making the full cast in the proper direction, or as near thereto as the wind will allow after relifting from the water. It will sometimes be found in making this manœuvre, and on other occasions when a false cast is necessary (*e.g.* to avoid obstructions, etc.), that the fly catches up on the line : this result is due to line and fly following the same path during their backward and forward flight, and may be avoided by taking care to make the false cast as far as may be possible from the line of the ultimate destination of the fly.

If a strong wind blows from behind it may also often be more convenient to switch, of which more will be written later, than to cast overhead, but when the wind blows in the opposite direction switching is of no help.

In an upstream wind one is forced to cut down into it, otherwise the breeze takes charge, line and fly are blown with the wind, and the whole cast, besides being of very moderate length, is blown quite out of fishing order. During such weather conditions it is better to take the line during the upward lift rather more in front of the angler by keeping the arms extended to some degree outwards, for if it be taken back in normal fashion danger exists of the wind carrying it down and inflicting damage to clothes, person, and temper, besides quite spoiling the attempt to cast. In bringing the rod forward, the point should be brought down lower and much more sharply than usual, while at the same time it should be directed so far as may be possible into the wind. The line is thus cut down and is not allowed to fall off with the wind, though it may be, at the expense of rather more disturbance to the surface of the water than is usual.

A very material aid to this 'cutting down' process, and indeed to all casts against the wind, is to reverse the hands. That is, in fishing from the left bank of the river from over the right shoulder the left hand is placed uppermost on the rod. By doing this one is able to pull the rod down and drag the line with it instead of pushing it down and causing the line to follow it, as in the more orthodox grip. In fact, this change of grip may be used as often as fancy dictates, because it gives a most valuable rest to some of the muscles in constant use without in any way adding to the difficulty or detracting from the efficiency of casting. Personally, I find I can often cast farther with this than with the normal grip.

A form of overhead cast in common use when difficulties such as trees or a high bank are present behind the angler is sometimes known as the steeple cast. In this the whole of the backward cast partakes more of an upward flick designed to carry the fly high into the air, the rod is checked rather earlier than usual, so that at no time does it pass the vertical, and no pause is made to allow the line to extend backwards. While the motion is continuous, timing must be almost more accurate than in the normal cast, and the movement must pass quite smoothly and evenly from the backward to the forward motion. If any jerk is made, a crack like that of a whip will be heard, and unless the gut be fairly thick, another fly will have joined the multitude that will be used no more. Anglers who habitually fish rivers where banks and other obstructions exist behind and above them very often use this form of cast exclusively, and are very pretty and effective fishermen.

When a short line suffices, a wonderful rest can be obtained by holding the rod with both hands above the reel, one on the wood and the other on the cork. The rod then is naturally not so powerful, but is surprisingly light to hold.

When bushes, bank, and trees are too close to be avoided by steeple casting, it may still be possible to fish effectively by using either a switch or a Spey cast, of which several variations in form exist. In all these casts the gut and fly are not lifted into the air, but merely drawn into a different position in the water ; they are allowed to remain in the water, and from there are projected anew across the stream.

In its most simple form this type of cast is used in flicking out the line until sufficient is extended to enable a proper cast to be made. Very quickly even the beginner will learn that it is easier to put out the first few yards by drawing in the hands, and then extending them forward, at the same time first raising and then thrashing down the rod point. This is the most elementary form of switch, and after a little practice it can soon be developed into a full-blown cast which, however, will never be as long as those made by other methods. With a moderate length of line out, the rod is sharply raised to the vertical, without, however, bringing line and fly out of the water, at the same time both hands are lifted slightly. A very short pause is made, and the rod point is then brought down smartly, both hands at the same time are allowed first to travel slightly forward in the direction of the throw and then brought back to the normal position. Not long ago I was watching a man switching a very long line with a trout rod and, being opposite the end of the line, I was much struck by its behaviour. As the fisher raised his rod, line and fly were drawn smartly through the water, then stopped dead, and remained without a move while one heard the thrash of the cast, and for an appreciable time thereafter. When the impetus imparted by the rod had travelled along the line, that part before me was suddenly whisked into the air and urged forward to the full extension of the cast. It was an illuminating example of switch casting at its best, and brought out its simplicity exceedingly well.

The real difficulty in switching is to be found in changing the direction of the cast through the angle (which can only be comparatively small) between the original and the new direction. This can be learnt solely by experience. If fly catches in line in the forward throw, the point of the rod during the second part of the cast should be held farther upstream.

For the Spey cast the procedure is rather different. It is really a development and refinement of the switch, sometimes almost a hybrid between it and an overhead cast, and provides not only a greater possible length of cast, but also more latitude in the direction of its delivery.

Instead of the fly being drawn only a short distance through the water, it is brought up past the front of the angler, either just clear of the water or actually along the surface by means, first of all, of an upward and outward movement of the rod to raise line and fly, and then a flick to bring them on their journey. Once above and clear of the angler they are allowed to fall back into the water, and the cast is continued practically in the motion of an overhead cast, starting from the point at which the rod then is (that is, not quite vertical, and held rather outwards in an upstream direction) and without lifting the line in the air. From the left bank, with the right hand uppermost, the point is brought round and outside of the right shoulder—with the rod still out of the vertical in the upstream direction—and is then brought forward sharply and upright past the angler's right ear, and so down to the horizontal or a little beyond. The cast is thus in three parts : (1) The upstream lift, (2) the circular retrogressive motion, (3) the forward movement and thrash as for a full-sized switch. But it must be made smoothly throughout with a slight pause only after the first movement.

If it has been correctly performed, the slack held in the hand for shooting will be torn out through the rings, just as in the case of an overhead cast.

A good Spey cast is a delight to watch, and perhaps can be most easily performed in a river of the type of that which gives it name, and which by its rapidity of current prevents the line and fly from sinking too deep. If too far immersed, the upstream lift is apt to fail in its purpose or be only partially successful : if the cast be continued after the fly has been deposited only opposite to or below the angler, then a surgical operation for the removal of hook from clothes or skin will almost inevitably be necessary. During the making of the cast the downstream foot, that is the foot opposite to the working shoulder, should be rather in advance of the other (try how awkward it is to have them in the reverse position, or even parallel), and the rod should be gripped moderately firmly. When performed by an expert, the Spey cast is light and straight on the water, but in clumsy hands, and especially if overmuch force be used, it can cause quite considerable commotion. In this last event, less force should be used and aim should be made a little higher above the water.

If a rather strong wind be blowing downstream, and especially down and across the stream towards the angler, the straight forward Spey cast may become complicated, owing to the frequency with which a bight of the line is caught up by the hook, and to the fact that the angler himself is also in grave danger of being struck or hooked. A modification of the cast to meet this situation has been introduced. It is sometimes called the Double-Spey cast, but is in reality nothing but the ordinary Spey cast performed over the ' wrong,' *i.e.* the downstream, shoulder with the necessary modifications. The line is drawn up until the rod is held completely upright immediately in front of the angler's body, so as to bring the fly to rest a short distance below him. (When one becomes expert and has a long line out, it may be necessary to carry the rod to the upstream side of the angler to achieve the right position for the fly.) The point is then dropped in front of the angler, carried round outside and behind the downstream shoulder, and brought forward with an overarm motion close to the downstream ear, and so forward to the completion of the throw. This case may be carried out with the hands in the normal position on the rod, that is, they will be actually ' wrong ' when compared with the shoulder over which the action takes place, or they can be reversed with the downstream hand on top, in which event they will be ' right ' *vis-à-vis* the shoulder.

As was mentioned in the chapter on rods, the best weapon for Spey casting is a spliced greenheart with the top joint rather heavier than usual. The value of this ' action ' will be realized when the forward throw and downward cut is made, for it materially helps to pick the line up and project it forward. A split bamboo rod with an even action throughout and a comparatively fine top may do if one only wants to use this type of cast occasionally, but it is undeniably more difficult to learn with such a rod, which, moreover, is never so adequate or effective for the purpose as one of plain whole wood.

Chapter IV

FISHING A POOL

As soon as a very modest proficiency in casting has been obtained, the beginner will naturally want to try to catch a fish, and certainly for the first few essays a pool should be chosen with a nice even current throughout its breadth, and as far as possible throughout its length also. Slack water, and worse still an eddy, close to the bank makes fishing much more difficult.

At first nothing more can be done than to start as near to the top of the pool as is necessary, and fish down, with an interval of two yards or so between each cast, until all the holding water within reach has been covered. Effort should be made to get every cast out to an equal length, but if any one in particular be only moderately good, do not lift immediately and cast again : allow such a cast to fish out in the ordinary way, and then if necessary make another and better effort to cover the outer water. An indifferent cast very often gets a fish, and if the line be somewhat slack, the chances of hooking one that takes the fly are materially increased. Ghillies somewhat naturally take pride in their casting, and sometimes are a little apt to be too impatient with casts which are not absolutely perfect in their length and alignment.

At first also it will be well to adopt the standard advice of casting at an angle of approximately 45 degrees to the stream. Not only does this reduce to a minimum the angle through which the change of alignment has to be made, but it also provides the easiest and most simple run for the line and fly.

34

As soon as some experience has been gained, refinements will naturally present themselves as necessary. For instance, it will be found that in rather fast water and especially if the faster water be nearer the bank, a ' belly ' is apt to form in the line in the downstream direction. Very little imagination is required to realize that not only must the fly be dragged very fast across the current with a final flip as the line straightens out, but that in extreme cases many fish will have an excellent opportunity of seeing both the line and the whole of the cast before the fly is presented to them, and presented, moreover, head first. This may be corrected directly the cast is made by lifting the rod point to an angle of about 30 degrees above the horizontal and carrying it and as much line as it can conveniently lift in an upstream direction. This manoeuvre will draw as much of the line as possible into proper alignment with the stream, but it is obvious that in doing so the fly will be moved through the water for as great a distance as the rod is moved upstream, without any chance of attracting fish. The drawback may be overcome if some of the slack line in the hand is released, or sufficient is pulled off the reel, and the whole of the line as far down as may be necessary is held clear of the water, and lifted over in the desired direction by a gentle switching motion. Like so many other things in fishing, ' lifting over ' or ' switching over ' is much more easily demonstrated than described, and once the effect of the downstream belly has been observed and the idea of the corrective mastered, the exact action necessary for its execution will soon be acquired with a little practice.

A little observation will show that considerable difference exists between anglers in the handling of the rod while the fly is in the water. Some do not move it at all ; others waggle it gently ; the extreme is reached on the Irish Erne, where the

' Ballyshannon waggle ' causes the rod to vibrate powerfully and fast from end to end.

In fast water it is better not to move the rod at all. The current itself imparts enough movement to the fly to attract fish, and too much movement only helps to make them miss it when they rise. In a slow current also, especially in early spring fishing, no movement may be most effective, but in warmer water some move may help to attract fish and prevent them turning away too easily satisfied as to the fly's identity.

If movement be desired, gently waving the rod top will not produce the required result. The slack of the line takes up such attempts. A really marked effort is needed to ' work ' the fly.

When fishing down a pool, it is always necessary to keep a look out for likely ' lies ' for fish. In some pools, of course, with a much broken-up bottom and water neither too deep nor too shallow, fish may lie anywhere. In others, where the bottom is predominantly smooth or soft, or where great variations in depth occur, they are much more likely to be found at certain points than at others. A slight upwelling in the water, or a turn in the current from the general line may indicate a boulder, or shelf, or projecting point of rock, around which fish may lie. These points should receive more particular attention, and while the rest of the pool may be fished comparatively quickly on the cast-two-steps-and-cast principle, several casts may profitably be made without shifting the stance at and around these spots. Many experienced anglers are inclined to devote too little time to the most promising lies, and to pass on to what is really more mediocre water, if a fish does not come at the first, or at the most at the second, cast.

Only when one is fishing with a greased line, or in clear and rather still water, or has an observer watching from a suitable eminence, does one learn how many fish may actually rise to the fly, and

how many more may follow it for a longer or
shorter distance, without in either case breaking
the water or touching the lure. All these fish
are potential takers, and given the knowledge of
their first move, it is often possible to induce
them to make a second or subsequent more serious
attempt by continuing to cast, either with the
same fly or with another size, or very occasionally
with another pattern. When one is fishing deeper
or in faster and rougher water, there is no reason to
suppose that any fewer fish move to the fly, or that
given that knowledge any smaller proportion of
these might be caught if the casts were repeated.

Probably, therefore, the most useful way to fish
a pool is to cover the apparently less useful parts
somewhat rapidly, and to concentrate rather more
than ordinary attention on the spots which are
obviously promising, or are reported to be good
lies for fish.

If a careful watch is kept, just a sight of the tip
of a tail or an unnatural move on the surface of the
water will often give the clue to a fish which has
moved. When such has been the case, there are
two schools of thought as to the subsequent procedure. The one advises that continued efforts
should be made immediately, first with the fly
which excited the fish's curiosity, and then with
others. The second suggests that waiting tactics
should be adopted, for an appreciable time (" a pipe
should be smoked " is the old adage, though how
we non-smokers are to note the passing of time is
not explained), and then the fish again attacked
with the same fly. Probably both schools are
right.

If the fish has merely had a look, continued
casting may produce the desired result, indeed,
steady casting at one point, without splash or other
disturbance, can sometimes induce even a lethargic
fish to take. I remember on one occasion watching
an angler with a prawn go out on to a branch of

a tree overhanging the water. From this vantage point he dropped his prawn about a couple of inches in front of a salmon lying in the gin-clear water just below, and he then moved the prawn up and down quite slowly and gently. At first that salmon frankly was not at all interested, then one saw the fins move slightly, as did the tail also; the movements became more definite, and finally the fish opened his mouth and wholeheartedly went for the prawn, with the result that it was firmly hooked. Whether fly would have had the same effect I cannot say, but it is certain that this fish had no intention of taking a lure, and was definitely irritated into so doing.

If on the other hand the fish has been scared by an unnatural movement of the fly, brought about through either an unfortunate vagary of the water or an equally unfortunate twitch or drag on the line by the angler, it is better to allow it to have time to rest and recover its somewhat shattered nerves while another bit of water is fished or the procrastinating pipe is smoked. Curiously enough, this unnatural movement of the fly has a far more frightening effect than has a slight prick from the hook.

A very lightly pricked fish will often, and one that has been harder hit will sometimes, come again immediately. A scared fish will seldom even rise a second time, though I remember on one occasion an exception to this rule. I had caught one fish from a very narrow lie close in to the bank and, starting to fish again, had not expected another from the same spot, so lifted the fly rather quickly, with the result that it was snatched away from a fish which rose to it. I gave it a rest and cast again. That fish desperately wanted the fly, but was like a child with burnt fingers. It was about the shyest fish on earth, rose eight or nine times all round the fly, but finally decided the game was not worth the candle and gave it up. Unfortunately

the immediate necessity for a long journey prevented
me trying it again after a second and longer rest.

A view of the angler will sometimes make fish
very shy, in fact it may thoroughly frighten them,
though in this respect fish of different rivers seem
to vary to an extraordinary degree. In parts of the
Aberdeenshire Dee for instance, when the water
is not too high and the light is right, one can
see a large proportion of the fish in perhaps three-
quarters of the width of the river. Those close in
to one's own bank may move quietly farther out,
but the rest apparently pay no attention. Wading
down slowly and quietly on to them, they also
seem not to be alarmed until one is rather past
them and getting outside their range of vision,
when they will swim upstream away from one.
In smaller rivers, on the other hand, I have often
seen the figure of an angler excite panic in a pool.
On the whole one should keep out of sight as far
as possible, move slowly and carefully and never,
if it can be avoided, get into a position where the
fish see one above their horizon and against the
sky.

Fish will often follow the fly round, and one
sometimes realizes this by the boil they make when
turning away on getting frightened at the shallow-
ness of the water. It is well, therefore, to be prepared for such behaviour, and unless the water be
very shallow indeed, the fly should be gently drawn
upstream when straight below the angler before it
is lifted for the next cast, or the angler moves
down in preparation for it.

The moment when the fly starts to move upstream
is very deadly for these following fish, I suppose
because they think that the curious object they have
been inspecting is moving away from them. The
first part of the movement, for a reason which will
shortly be stated, should come undoubtedly from
raising the rod point ; thereafter two or three
short portions of line may be pulled in through

the rings. In really favourable places it is better
if this recovery be made quite evenly and smoothly,
and not in a series of pulls. The even movement
seems to be more attractive to the fish, and may
be made by a series of turns of the hand, first palm
and then back being uppermost. Again, description
is more difficult than execution. One must imagine
first the palm uppermost and the line held by the
thumb and first finger, being nearest to the first
ring : the hand is then turned over, thumb and first
finger (still retaining their grip) towards the reel,
until the little finger can be raised sufficiently to
come on top of the line. This small finger is then
turned downwards with the line (thumb and first
finger still retaining their grip) until the palm is once
more uppermost, when the thumb and first finger
take a fresh grip and the movement is repeated.

The exact size of fly to be used can only be
learnt by experience : if it be too large the fish
may be scared, and if it be too small they may
take no notice of it. Perhaps one of the chief
controlling factors is the temperature of the water,
but the colour of the water, strength, and rough-
ness of the stream, and the depth and smoothness
or otherwise of the pool all play their part.

While the water remains below 38° F. spring
conditions may be said to prevail, and large flies
from $1\frac{3}{4}$ to 3 inches long are required. From
38° to 44° F. is a transition stage, when neither
the angler nor the fish seems to be able to make
up their minds as to the right size. $1\frac{1}{4}$ to $1\frac{1}{2}$ inches
may be the central selection, but fish may also be
caught with much larger and also smaller lures.
Above 44° F. summer conditions usually obtain,
and flies less than an inch long are of the greatest
use.

Fishing during various parts of the season is
dealt with in other chapters, but it would perhaps
be convenient to consider briefly here some general
ideas regarding the sizes of flies. When the water

J. Edwards Moss.

THE 'STEEPLE' CAST BY TOM SCOTT.
Note bank and position of hands and rod.

J. Edwards Moss.

THE WRONG WAY TO CAST BY THE AUTHOR.
Rod too far back.

is really cold, little trouble on this score need be experienced, for the fish are all lying in slack water of the same type, and all one can do is to get the fly down to them.

But as the water gets warmer and they progressively move into the more streamy portions and then into the rapid current, the question becomes more complicated. All experience suggests that comparatively little latitude is then allowable in the size of fly if the greatest success is to be obtained. Most anglers and ghillies appreciate this, and pick a fly to suit the general conditions of a pool which is to be fished, but comparatively few go farther. Yet if we consider the subject for a short time we begin to realize that even in the one pool very considerable variations may occur. For instance, if we take a certain pool known as the Two Stones Pool we find that at the top there is some very fast rough water where the somewhat narrow entering stream, so common to the Spey, comes down the rather steep divide from the water above : this stream gradually spreads and eases into the wider and deeper water of the pool proper, the upper portion of which can be fished in the summer. There is then slack water, ideal in spring but of little or no use in summer, and finally a smooth glide of rather shallow water below the stones, which give the pool its name, into the next run.

Here we have three different conditions ; at the top the very rough water ; in the middle the slackening stream, and below this the flowing water of the pool. It is obvious that the fly which is of the proper size for the first part is probably rather over large for the second, and certainly considerably too big for the last. It is also certain that the fly which will definitely attract fish out of the deeper pool may excite the curiosity of those in the tail glide up to a point, but will not be sufficiently attractive to be fatal to them.

To fish this pool properly, therefore, flies of at least three, and probably four, different sizes are required. A compromise might be reached by not changing the first fly until half-way down the second part, and then putting on one that would also do for the third portion, but it would probably not give the angler the best possible chance.

The reaction of a fish to a fly that is too big is either to rise short or to follow it, and the trouble is that in anything like streamy water it is often impossible to observe what the fish may be doing, and to apply the necessary corrective. Another cause of short rising, or following fish, particularly in summer, is that the fly is being fished too slowly.

On some occasions it may pay when fish are dour to fish a pool down with a fly that is obviously very much too big, and to follow this with another of the proper size. The large fly, if carefully fished without splashing, does not scare the fish, but awakens their interest, and they are then more ready for the lure of reasonable proportions. I have known one generous angler fish a big fly before breakfast without saying anything, so that an elderly and indifferent fishing guest might be as certain as possible of getting a fish when he started immediately after the meal. It had the happiest results.

When, however, one is fishing a pool down only once, it behoves one to take care to use not just a fly of approximately the right size, but one which is adapted for each part of the pool. The change is very easily and quickly made, and very soon after starting the necessary range of sizes is accumulated in the wet fly box, so that only if a different pattern is required does recourse have to be made to those dry in the fly boxes proper.

As well as varying the size of fly, it is also evident that a variation in the method of fishing must be made in the different parts of a pool. In the top rough stream every effort must be made by switching over and by holding the rod as far across the stream as possible to slow down the pace of the fly so that fish may have a chance of seeing and taking the fly, and not merely have it swept past them by the weight of water on the line. In the slower stream current conditions will probably be just right to work the fly without any unusual precautions on the part of the angler, but as the pool proper is reached head work may again be necessary. Here, effort will be required, not to slow the fly, but to hasten its passage so that it does not hang and droop, and so that fish do not see too much of it. This may be accomplished by leaving some degree of downstream belly in the line, or by pulling the line in through the rings by hand, with the result that as the fly swings slowly down with the current it is also deliberately drawn across by mechanical action.

By this last manœuvre quite still water may be fished with as much success as the most ideal stream. At first it may be somewhat difficult to judge accurately the best pace at which to move the fly, though the fish will soon show their approval or disapproval of the speeds which are tried. At first, too, if a fish takes when the fly is near the end of its journey some embarrassment will be felt from the coils of loose line held in the hand. Unless pressed, a newly hooked fish is very often quiet for a time and, while holding line against it with one hand, the slack can be reeled in with the other, or line may be partly yielded and partly taken up. In any case this question of slack will be found to be not nearly so serious in practice as it sounds in theory.

One real difficulty to many people fishing slack water, however, is that of getting out the whole length of line again after each cast. If the water is wide and necessitates bringing the fly in on quite a short line after each cast, this can only be done by one or more false casts. These should be made so as to avoid as far as is possible disturbing the fish, and in such a direction that the final cast will be clear, and that no danger will exist of the hook catching up on the line. This last trouble will occur if the false cast is made in a direction too closely approximating to that of the final cast.

Undoubtedly the ideal conditions for angling are to be found when the water has cleared and fallen to a moderate size after a good flood. Other things being favourable, so long as it continues to fall without becoming too low, fishing should be good. The reason probably is either that fresh fish are in the river, or those already there have been awakened to new life, they have run their course and are now in no hurry, so that they are quite prepared to take an interest in things around them.

With a rising water, however, it is different. Fish are then eager and expectant. They want to get on, to get over obstructions, and to complete another stage in their journey. They do not care about lures or other trivialities.

The first half-hour of a rise, it is true, may be distinctly good. The fish then seem to be waking up but not yet on the move. Later in many places angling is almost, if not quite, hopeless, though an odd fish resting for a very short time may sometimes be picked up in a good lie but rather out of the main current when the water is rough. Perhaps more than one may be obtained in a pool, and more especially in the tail of a pool, situated in a position where the fish have a long tiring run without possibility of rest before they can reach it. But in good, deep water without any particular difficulty to face, they pass on without halt or hesitation, and the angler there who, in these circumstances, packs up and goes home, will not miss much sport.

If all anglers would continue to do as no doubt
they started, and only respond to the pull of a
fish by striking after a slight delay, far more fish
would be hooked and landed than is the case at
present.

Normally a salmon moves to the fly comparatively
slowly even in fast water, as may be easily seen in
certain clear water rivers. Occasionally, of course,
it may take a fly in a hurry when it has to, or when
sufficiently excited, but usually it sees it from some
distance off, slowly moves into action, rises above
the fly whether that be near the surface or deep
in the water, opens its mouth and takes the fly on
its downward path, then turns sideways and downstream in order to return to its original lie.

It is not like a trout, which has to take the natural
insects when and how it can, nor is it like them in
expecting something soft and non-resistant. A
salmon fly is not alarming to a salmon even when
it chews it, provided it feels no pull or resistance
from the line, nor is it prepared to spit it out without
further ado. Once resistance is felt it is altogether
another matter, but the longer one can wait without
putting on strain before striking, the greater will be
the chances of securely hooking the fish. At first,
unless it has been able to get a very generous
grasp, it will in all probability only have the fly
at the end of the jaws, and on striking the hook
will only hit the bone or the skin thereabouts—
later, from the result of the turning movement, the
fly may be well back in the mouth.

One famous angler, now unfortunately no longer
with us, tried the experiment with a greased line
in fairly slack water of exerting no pressure at all
after the fish rose. He found that the fly was
passed out through the gills, and that ultimately
he played the fish with the hook in its side and the
cast leading through the gills and out of its mouth !
A parallel is to be found in the manner in which a
bunch of lobworms on a large hook and thick gut

will be passed down the gullet of a salmon if time
be given for the purpose.

The worst strike of all is, of course, that made
directly the fish is seen. That usually has only
one result—a lost and thoroughly scared fish.
Another bad strike is that made after the fish is
seen to rise, and when it is judged to have gone
down far enough to reach the fly. This usually
results only in a pull or a lightly hooked fish. One
should undoubtedly wait until the fish is actually
felt at the end of the line. If, when it is seen to
rise, slack can be given without disturbing the
fly, as is the case when a greased line is used,
so that when the fly is seized the fish may continue
its journey to the bottom and begin to turn before
the line is tightened, and the strike made, the
chances of a secure hold will be immeasurably
increased. To secure this end, one angler of my
acquaintance always holds a yard or so of slack in
his hand and lets this go when he sees or feels
a fish rise. He says that he undoubtedly now
hooks a far greater number in proportion to the
rises he gets than he did before he adopted this
stratagem.

The probability of hooking and landing a salmon
when it takes a fly at the end of a quite taut line is
slender, and particularly is this the case if the rod
be held low and there be little or no spring between
the fly and the angler's hand which is holding
the line. This is especially true towards the end
of a cast when the fly is almost directly downstream of the angler, when there is no suspicion
even of belly on the line, and when the fish is
taking the fly not at an angle but from directly
downstream of the bend of the hook. Unless
the point happens to get in right at the front angle
of the lower jaw, there is little to offer resistance
to it, and only a slight scrape is likely to result,
' a slight pull ' that is, such as we so often experience
with a rise made in these circumstances.

In order to anticipate this and avoid the unfortunate result, the rod point should be gradually raised as the fly comes round, so that both the bag in the line and the spring of the rod may provide some slack and buffer to allow the fish at least to get down, and if possible to begin to turn. The yard of loose line given from the hand is then also excellent, and if, when the rise is seen, the line is allowed to go as slack as possible, the prospect of getting the fish is very much more promising.

When spinning, of course, it is rather different. The rise is not then seen, and the line is normally taut. The fish feels the pull on the bait as soon as the latter is in its mouth, and no doubt given the chance would open its jaw, and the bait would be both ejected and withdrawn by the line. A quick strike when spinning is usually necessary.

In spring, when using large flies with points of corresponding proportions to the hooks and strong gut, a good hearty strike is required to pull the hook in over the barb. Half-measures are then of no use. But as hooks get smaller less effort is required to drive them home, or incidentally to break the cast. With the small hooks of late spring and summer, no strike in the ordinary sense of the word is necessary. Merely to hold the rod point up and let the weight of the fish pull on the line is quite sufficient to fix the hook firmly. More force is both superfluous and liable to cause a break.

Normally, being hooked does not scare a salmon. One would therefore think that it feels little or no pain. This may be proved if one lets the line go slack immediately after striking. The fish then stays where it is. I once had a most fortunate illustration of this fact. I had a lot of slack line in my hand, and just as I cast this went foul. No sooner had I thought of the predicament than a fish seized the fly. I had a yard or two of line available, and dropped both it and the rod point, expecting a smash. But the fish stayed quite still, nor did it move until I had the whole of the mess straightened out and the line again in order— a matter, I suppose, of two or three minutes. I was wading and one of the more amusing sides of the occasion was the expression and the movement of the anxious ghillie on the bank, who, only too willing to help, was yet unable to get to me.

It is the pull of the line, not the hold of the hook, which frightens the fish. To be taken off an even keel is one thing no self-respecting salmon will tolerate. Even in guddling salmon (after the manner of trout) they allow themselves to be drawn un-resisting from their lies, tail first, providing they are kept absolutely level, but once any lifting or move of that sort is attempted it is quite another story !

When playing a fish the old instruction to the beginner was to hold his rod up. The intention of this is to keep a bend in the rod so that its spring is available as a buffer. But if vertical, the rod has not only to pull against the fish, it has also to bear part of its weight if, as it naturally does, the fish puts its head down. With the fish a long way off, the rod has to be held up to keep the line from being ' drowned ' (that is, so much of the line is in the water that it is dragged after the fish beneath the surface, and does not follow it freely in the air with only a minimum amount under water). When the fish is near the angler, however, it is better to hold the rod horizontal, not pointing at, but roughly parallel with, the fish so that a sideways pull is exerted and the fish cannot take the strain by ' standing on its head.' This position is particu-larly valuable when a fish is being beached. Then also the angler should get as far from the water edge as possible by walking backwards. He should never, unless compelled by his surroundings, stand close and reel up to bring the fish through the last bit of water.

J. E. Davis.

LONG POOL, RIVER AURLAND, NORWAY.

If a fish be on the far side of a rather fast-running river, and the angler in his proper position (opposite to, or slightly below, the fish), it can very often be brought right over to the gaff very quickly once it starts to give way. Directly the fish's head is slightly turned so that the current is bearing on the far side of it, the angler, even if fishing with fine tackle, should reel as hard and fast as possible without a moment's cessation or slackening. Usually the combined pressure of water on one side and line on the other will prove too much, and the fish will ' otter ' right over until it is in the slack water, or actually in the shallows at the angler's feet.

Sometimes a fish sulks. Very often this is the angler's fault because he has allowed it to rest, or to get below him. Sulking usually means that the fish is almost vertical, with its head down, and in such a position that the rod cannot exert a side pull on it. Often a few fairly large stones, well aimed but thrown so as not to hit the cast, will dislodge it. Holding the rod vertical, the line as tight as possible, and then giving the button some vigorous blows may also be effective. In an extreme case a messenger sent down the line may produce quite a surprising activity. The invaluable chicken rings with a stone attached form excellent messengers. Some recommend a bunch of keys, though personally I would prefer to make sure that I had duplicates of all before putting them to this use.

In spite of all instructions and the angler's best endeavours, a fish will sometimes not only get downstream, but also into such a position that it cannot be followed. Brute force (somewhat a remedy of despair) or ' walking up ' are then the only resources available. In walking up, the reel must be kept absolutely silent, and the fish led upstream by the exercise of gentle pressure and a steady though slow walk. Once started, fish may sometimes be taken for a comparatively long distance in this manner, but they are often difficult to start.

If walking up be impossible, or the fish is heading for disaster without hope of getting on even terms with it, sometimes it can be stopped and turned upstream by letting line down so that the stream bears on the line and pulls at the fish from below. In an emergency, however, there must be nothing half-hearted in the way one sets about trying this method. The line must literally be torn off the reel yards at a time and urged into the water with the rod point. To be slow is to court certain failure.

Sometimes we are plagued with a series of ' short rises,' fish which show or just touch the fly (heaven knows how they do it so often without getting hooked), and perhaps some anglers are more prone to this particular annoyance than others. In certain districts also fish are said to be especially given to this particular habit.

Except in some very special and occasional conditions of light and atmosphere, it is hard to believe that any such thing as a naturally short rising fish exists. In the light of all the available evidence we can but accept as fact that salmon do not feed in fresh water : exceptional fish which swallow salmon parr, March Browns, or May flies, may exist, but they only suffice to prove the rule.

Why, therefore, a salmon takes a lure, or what it considers it to be, is the more difficult to understand. Whether, however, it be a relic or a forerunner of its sea appetite (we know that fresh-run fish and returning kelts are the most free risers), an exhibition of curiosity or anger, or merely an interlude in relief of sheer boredom, we can be certain that practically every fish starts out with the idea of investigating the object so closely that only actually mouthing it will satisfy its intention. If it does not proceed as far then either its curiosity or its anger (both would seem to be reasonable explanations when a fish takes a lure after repeated and continuous presentation) are satisfied, its budding appetite is quenched by what it is able to see of the lure, or it is scared by some part of the tackle.

A lure that is too large or, what amounts to the same thing, one that is fished too slowly, are certainly definite deterrents which can easily be put to the test of appropriate counter-action. A cast that is too thick where it joins the fly is also most certainly an inhibitive factor of far more frequent and potent occurrence than is commonly supposed. Salmon as well as trout are most definitely gut shy, and a series of most willing fish can be surely deterred, even when the fly is right, if the cast be overheavy.

At a certain famous loch fishing the proportion of fish hooked to those risen is extraordinarily small. It seems significant that the majority of anglers there use casts of the sizes known to tackle-makers as ' light salmon.' Several sizes finer would be much more appropriate to the surroundings, and, one would think, might well provide consider-ably better results, except on the occasions when a very strong wind indeed is blowing.

In fine fishing a tapered cast should always be used, and the end part can be quickly adjusted to any moderate alteration of requirement by adding a couple of links of finer gut, or removing the finest and leaving the fly to be attached to the next thicker stage. If a number of short rises are experi-enced and change of size of fly effects no improve-ment, the cast should always be regarded with grave suspicion.

Unduly heavy casting and splashing will make fish shy if it does not put them down altogether. When the water is smooth, every effort should be made to cast lightly and carefully.

A method which is rather the reverse of fine,

light casting but which, under certain circumstances is sometimes equally effective, is known
as dabbling.   This consists of allowing the fly
only, or with it at the most but an inch or two
of gut, to be on the surface and to ' skate ' so as
to create a definite disturbance and wake.   It is a
manœuvre which can only be performed on water
within easy reach of the rod, and which requires
either a strong upstream wind or a strong stream.
If the wind be blowing, the rod point is held well
up and the line allowed to belly so that the variation
in the strength of the air current drags the fly here
and there, sometimes at speed, sometimes slowly,
along the surface.   The same effect can be produced in a stream, but in this case it is perhaps
easier if a big fly be used as a sea anchor at the
end of the cast, and a dropper fly of the proper
size be used for the actual fishing.

In a loch salmon will also sometimes come freely
to a dropper fished in this manner.   In a river it
is absolutely necessary that a definite wake be
created.

One of the trials of spring fishing with the fly
as near the bottom as possible, or of spinning, is
that the lure, occasionally or frequently according to
the type of river, gets hung up on some obstruction.
In this event the hook normally enters from the
downstream side so that pulling from where one
is fishing in the upstream direction only results
in driving the hook home farther unless the obstruction be of a character that can be pulled away.
If the hold be on a rock, and it is extraordinary
how a grip is obtained in a minute hole or below
an almost imperceptible ledge, a straight pull
properly delivered may, however, be effective.
In this case the rod should be put right down,
the line pulled in through the rings until dead
taut, an extra pull (within the breaking strain of
the cast, of course) given, and the slack line immediately allowed to fly free.   The spring resulting

from this often causes the hook to jump off its position.

In the case of a more definite fixture, some yards of line should be pulled off the reel and a loop of line switched downstream of the obstruction. This free line should be allowed to settle in the water so that it has some resistance, and then a smart pull should be given by the rod point. The theory is, of course, that the pull is passed through the bend in the line and comes on to the hook from a downstream direction, and at least partly, if not wholly, from the direction taken by the hook in striking the snag or whatever it may be.

If several switches do not result in a free hook, then a bottle or ' floater ' must be used to help. An empty corked bottle or floater is made fast by a piece of twine to one of those coloured rings which are used to put on the legs of domestic fowls to distinguish age, breeding, and so on. This ring is then threaded on to the line beyond the rod point and the rod held up so that the ring and with it the bottle or floater first runs free down the line until it strikes the water. With the line held moderately taut, it will continue its passage downstream along the line until, when it is within a few yards of the obstruction, slack should be given so that it passes beyond the hold. A downstream pull can then be delivered from the rod more effectively than is possible with merely a loop of line switched over.

In the case of an obstinate entanglement, the float can be tried in various positions either directly at, or considerably below, the position of the hook. Finally, if nothing remains but a break, the rod point is put down and the line pulled in by hand or held while the angler walks backwards.

If a fly be caught in a tree, help may be obtained from a metal hook or forked stick, attached to a strong piece of twine and inserted in the end ring of the rod. The hook or stick is then placed in position on the offending branch by the rod, the rod is withdrawn, and either branch or hook (or both) drawn down by pulling on the twine attached to the hook or stick. If a shot gun be handy a branch that is not too thick may be shot down.

CHAPTER V

HOOKS AND FLIES

This is not the place in which to enter into the history of the use and development of the artificial fly for the capture of salmon. Others have done that far better than I could, and it is now sufficient to say that the use of flies is by no means only a modern practice. Salmon angling is mentioned in the first book on fishing (*A Treatyse of Fysshynge wyth an Angle*) at the end of the fifteenth century, and flies (of unknown dressing) were evidently one of the less popular lures of that time. Succeeding authors in the historical literature of the subject continue to refer to this form of fishing but, according to Mr. Taverner, it was not until 1826 that the actual dressing for any particular pattern of fly was printed. Mr. Taverner was, however, able to obtain from Messrs. Allcock a pattern fly of the date 1775, which seems to give evidence of some considerable development in the art of fly dressing even at that date. This fly was not only complicated, as are many of our modern patterns, by a body consisting of a variety of colours, but had also a tag of flat silver tinsel. It is interesting to note that the larger sizes of early flies seem to have covered their nakedness not with one long wing, but with a series of two or even three wings set tandem-wise, the one behind the other. At that time probably the practicability of the use of long feather fibres for wings had not been realized.

But enough of history. Let us turn to the modern fly and the basis on which it is built, the hook, pausing only for one moment to notice the various methods of attachment between fly and cast.

The earliest hooks had a straight plain shank, to which a length of twisted hair was whipped, the hair in turn being made fast to the cast by a knot or loop. In due course the hair was replaced by a length of gut and later still by a gut loop. About the date of the invention of this last there seems to be some doubt. Mr. Taverner is inclined to treat a reference to an eye in 1845 as a metal eye on the hook, but since Stoddart only a few years later, in his *Anglers' Companion*, refers to a loop of gut at the head of the hook as a recent improvement, it is more than likely that the 1845 reference was to the same thing. In any case, if metal eyes for salmon hooks had been in existence at that time, it is likely that a similar hook for trout would have ante-dated Mr. Hall's hook of 1875.

It is more than probable that metal eyes for salmon hooks post-dated similar hooks for trout, but it is certain that they have only come into general use within recent years. Up to the 1914–1918 War the majority of salmon flies were still dressed on hooks with gut loops whipped on, and it is only within the next five or ten years that the eye hook gained the ascendancy. Various objections have been, and sometimes still are, raised against the modern form. It is said that the direct joint between metal eye and cast is unsound, that the eye is clumsy, that the fly does not swim properly, and so on. It seems certain that the gut loop on the fly provides a buffer connection between metal hook and cast, but what particular advantage this may convey is much more doubtful. In the course of continuous fishing the cast perhaps is not quite so liable to ' neck ' at the point of tying in, but this defect with metal eyes can be easily corrected by sacrificing a minute portion of the cast and retying it occasionally.

It seems to me that the modern metal eye is

rather less clumsy than the gut eye, and certainly no effect is exerted by either of the two on the manner in which a fly swims in the water. Normally a fly is kept on an even keel by the pull of the line, but even if the line goes slack, the extra weight of the point and bend inevitably take it down tail first. On the score of length of life and safety there can be no two opinions. The life of the gut in a gut eye is in reality no greater than that of a cast, although a certain preliminary super-abundance of strength may make its apparent life longer. A loop may also be ' necked ' at the joint with metal, while the rest of the gut is still strong, and a loop may ' draw ' from the hook owing to bad or old tying. Certain substitutes, e.g. violin strings, have sometimes been used, to mitigate the defects of necking and loss of strength. A fly on a metal-eyed hook, on the other hand, is good and safe as long as the hook lasts and enough of the original dressing remains to attract the fish (it is surprising how much may be lost without detriment).

While approving in the most complete manner of metal-eyed hooks, one has to make certain criticisms of some of them. Far too many are made of wire that is unnecessarily heavy, with the result that the whole hook is clumsy and the eye entirely objectionable. This is a particularly bad fault in the medium and small sizes with which the use of a comparatively fine cast is necessary. In this case the gut necks both surely and quickly, and the whole effect is bad.

Except in the very smallest sizes, approximating to trout fly size, a bad fault is for the wire of the eye merely to be turned back against the shank of the hook—at the best it is apt to fray the gut, and at the worst the gut will slip through the gap. The loop should be formed by the wire being returned along the shank, and nicely tapered so as to fit snugly to it. To the layman no reason seems to

5

exist why a neat loop of wire of appropriate section should not be formed before the whole is tempered. Each hook is hand-made and formed while the wire is in a soft and pliable condition. Manufacturers seem to think that for a big fish one must have a heavy hook ; they do not appear to realize that any hook, large or small, properly made and tempered, of the finest wire which may reasonably be used, must be considerably stronger than the greatest pull one can exert with a rod, or which the cast employed with the hook will stand.

In recent years certain hook-makers have endeavoured to overcome the heavy eye by making the hook as for the old-fashioned gut loop, and brazing thereon a metal eye of wire finer than that used for the hook. The idea is excellent, and the hook produced has an altogether pleasing appearance.

That is one grievance against the hook-makers. Another is the multiplicity of mystic scales which they use to indicate the size of their hooks, and the lack of absolute uniformity even when one particular scale is employed. The obvious and sensible method of measuring a hook is from the outside of the bend to the end of the shank (*i.e.* the overall measurement) excluding the eye in the case of metal-eyed hooks. It is that least employed, and in point of fact has only been introduced by Dr. T. E. Pryce-Tannatt under the name of the Rational Scale in quite recent years. Under this scale the larger hooks have an interval of $\frac{1}{4}$ inch ; this is gradually decreased until in the smallest sizes likely to be used for salmon, the difference between each number is only $\frac{1}{16}$ inch.

The scale most in use is the Limerick or Old Scale. In this there is a change of notation at $1\frac{3}{8}$ inches. From this size downwards the sizes are designated by numbers in an ascending scale, and in the smallest sizes there are approximately four numbers in each complete quarter inch :

numbers 1 to 4 include $1\frac{1}{4}$ inches to $\frac{15}{16}$ inch inclusive, but numbers 7 to 10, $\frac{3}{4}$ inch to $\frac{9}{16}$ inch inclusive.

From $1\frac{1}{2}$ inches to larger sizes the numbers are also indicated in numerical order, but in this case before a stroke and cypher. Thus a hook $1\frac{1}{2}$ inches long is number 1/0, and to 2 inches, which is number 5/0, the interval between each size is $\frac{1}{8}$ inch. After 5/0 the interval becomes $\frac{1}{4}$ inch, and the largest normal size is number 10/0 or $3\frac{1}{4}$ inches. But in this original scale the whole hook gradually increased in proportion all round, so that the larger sizes became really formidable weapons, with no inconsiderable gape between point and shank, necessitating the use of relatively thick wire. To overcome to some extent this defect the length of shank was increased at certain sizes without a corresponding increase in gape. These hooks are sometimes referred to as Dee hooks, and were made at least as early as 1850 ; after 4/0 (approximately $1\frac{3}{4}$ inches), 5/0 was omitted and instead of 6/0 another size designated $4/0\frac{1}{4}$ (2 inches) and meaning a 4/0 gape with a shank $\frac{1}{4}$ inch longer than that size was formed. Number $4/0\frac{1}{2}$ means an increase of a further $\frac{1}{4}$ inch, and there are also additions of $\frac{1}{2}$ inch to the 5/0 and 6/0 sizes.

Some hooks are black, others bronzed colour, and some even are plated on the ground that, reflecting light, they are less visible to the fish. These last I have never tried. The bronzed hooks are said by some to be harder tempered than the black and consequently more easily broken against a rock or on the bone of a fish's mouth. Be this as it may (so far as I am aware, no definite proof exists in either direction) it is advisable to test each hook, whether one buys them bare and dresses them oneself, or the flies are bought complete. The point, which should be needle sharp, should be inserted in a block of soft wood and a sharp pull given to the eye—an undertempered hook will not

recover its original shape with dispatch, and one
seriously overtempered will snap.

A great deal of discussion takes place from time
to time as to the ideal shape for the hook and the
best form of point and barb. Nowadays the conventional shape of a salmon hook has settled down
into the Limerick bend, or a slight modification
thereof. Its very general use would suggest that
it is best, and certainly for the large sizes and
Dee hooks it seems to be eminently satisfactory.
For the smaller sizes I personally prefer a round bend
hook, beloved of many old anglers who have
described it to me as the Cork bend, which it is
now almost impossible to obtain. The bend was
reproduced in perfection in the Illingworth hooks
(now unobtainable), and certainly my experience
has been that hooks of this bend are better ' holders '
than any others. *De faut de mieux*, one has now to
buy the Limerick hooks, but among these one
should search for a brand having a gape as wide
as possible.

Whether the eye be upturned or downturned is
of no moment, nor so far as I have discovered is a
slight upturning of the shank in some makes of
the larger sizes of any importance. A personal
preference for the downturned eye is purely an
admission of incompetence, as I dress my own flies
and find it easier to tie in the wings with no eye in
the way.

John Bickerdyke (the late Wm. Cook), probably
in the 'nineties of last century, invented a long shank,
short-dressed, double-hooked fly which he called
the Salmo Irritans fly which had no great popularity,
but during the last ten years a vogue for long-
shank single hooks in the smaller sizes has been
started.

On these the fly is not dressed full length, but a
portion of the shank is left projecting beyond the
tag, and the bend is relatively some distance behind
the fly. The idea, which if not originating from,

was fostered and developed by, the late Mr. A. H. E.
Wood, is that some of the so-called short rising
fish would be hooked, and those that appear merely
to nip the tail of the fly would find more of the
business part of the lure in their mouths. This may
be so, but I have never been able to convince
myself that it is the case although I naturally defer
to the opinions and experience of Mr. Wood. I
have definitely noticed, however, that more fish
seem to be lost after hooking with these hooks
than with the ordinary short shanks, and especially
if the latter be accompanied by a round bend.
Most clearly was this the case with a certain brand
of these long-shank hooks made of nice light wire,
but of a rather springy temper, so much so that
I discarded the whole lot and have never since
used them. Should anyone use these hooks they
should certainly choose those of a good ' solid '
temper with a minimum of spring in shank or
bend.

Various odd types of hook have been tried from
time to time, and among these perhaps the most
noteworthy are the so-called barbless in which the
barb is replaced by a bend in the form of a hump
in the wire. A great merit of these is that the point,
owing to the absence of the cut and shape of the
barb is needle-form and needle-sharp, and penetra-
tion is exceedingly easy. In my experience they hold
fish just as well as the normal type, and are very
useful if it be necessary to employ small sizes during
the smolt descent in April, May, and June : the
little fish can be unhooked very easily and without
any appreciable damage, which is not by any means
always the case with barbed hooks.

It might appear that in this chapter flies should
play a much more important part than hooks but,
in my opinion, comparatively little need be said
about the external trappings which ensnare both
anglers and fish. Of one thing I am convinced.
The list of available flies is absurdly and ridiculously

long, and the number of patterns carried by most
of us unnecessarily large. That the fish—the same
species of fish living under almost precisely the
same conditions—of one river should reject flies
preferred by those in another, or that in any one
district they could and would discriminate between,
say, a Wilkinson and a Silver Doctor, seems to me
to be both incomprehensible and improbable in
the extreme. Nor would it appear to be necessary
to use flies of almost an entirely different type under
similar conditions in Scotland, Ireland, and Newfoundland or the eastern side of Canada. It has
always seemed to me to be somewhat significant
that in the fashionable rivers where rents are high
only the most complicated and expensive flies are
reputed to be of any use, while in other districts
where the fishing costs little or nothing, and is
consequently engaged in chiefly by those of very
limited purses, the fish are said to favour only the
most simple flies, which may be dressed or bought
for a correspondingly low figure. One can hardly
believe that the fish so definitely and kindly note
the purses of their pursuers, and one may therefore
be excused some polite scepticism when told that
only this, that, or the other fly is of any use in a
particular river.

By all this I do not, of course, mean that any
one fly will be good at all times under all circumstances, even in its full range of sizes, and that no
advantage will be gained from some changes. It
would seem only reasonable that two distinct types
might provide a useful change, the one, say, with
a predominantly dull body, *e.g.* a Black Doctor,
and the other with an undoubtedly bright body,
e.g. a Silver Doctor. I do not intend to imply that
the two named are the only two, or that a Jock
Scott (beloved of all ghillies) or Green High-
lander, Wilkinson, or Silver Gray, or a dozen
other patterns of either type might not serve as
well.

It is difficult to believe that a fish appreciates all the subtleties and frills of the dressing of a Jock Scott or in three or four feet of dark peat-stained Thurso water is able to pick and choose between the ruby glories of Kate and the prawn-like make-up of a genuine Torrish of true descent.

In fact many, or most, of the flies in the tackle-makers' shops are so heavily dressed that much of the inherent properties of parts of the dressing are entirely masked and lost in a superabundance of material. From what we have been told and have learnt of the underwater appearance of flies, some at least of their attraction lies in the 'flash' which comes from parts of them. Even some of this quality may be lost in the overdressed specimens. When spread in the water the wings and hackle should be at least partially translucent, and should not mask the body and the flash coming from the tinsel on it. I have known of bought flies being severely pruned with a pair of scissors with much advantage.

Size, of course, is a matter quite apart from pattern. Of sizes one requires a full range. My advice to the beginner would be to restrict seriously the number of patterns in his first purchases, or first attempts at dressing, but that he should get an ample supply in the sizes which he is most likely to require for his fishing be it in spring, summer, or autumn. For patterns of the medium or larger sizes he may, as I have indicated, please himself without, in my opinion, interfering in the slightest degree with the success of his sport. Possibly even one pattern alone might not reduce his final bag materially, if at all. In the words, however, of the Scots proverb 'changes are lightsome,' and on a day when sport is dull, to change a fly is sometimes a variation to the fisherman if not to the fish.

If fishing strange water, one is often very much in the hands of the fisherman or ghillie who, although usually a most excellent man, can be wonderfully obstinate about the pattern of flies. If his favourite flies are not available, he is apt to react most unfavourably to the whole of the rest of the proceedings.

About dry flies for salmon no necessity exists to write anything, since no one has made any success of their use in British waters. Flies best adapted for greased line fishing and for general low water work will be mentioned in the chapters dealing with these special forms of angling.

Regarding hooks and flies, only one item remains for discussion, and that is the highly controversial subject of single versus double hooks. Of the respective and comparative merits of each there is no proof, and while one angler favours the one, another prefers the other. Personally I like the single hook the better, perhaps because I have given double hooks insufficient trial. Those in favour of them say that the two hooks (they usually confine their remarks to the smaller sizes) not only give a double chance of a grip, but also on many occasions provide actually a double hold. When required, the extra weight also helps the fly to swim lower in the water. The other school of thought expresses the opinion that not only may the double hook prevent the fish closing its mouth firmly on one hook but also when one has a grip the other may act as a lever in freeing it. It is a matter on which each individual angler has to take his own stand in the light of his experience or prejudice, but few, if any, advocate double hooks in the larger sizes. Some of the smallest size double hooks are to be found with a very bad fault, the eye neither up-turned nor down-turned, but in a straight line with the shank. To this eye it is not only difficult to attach the cast satisfactorily, but a break after a fish is hooked only too frequently happens.

CHAPTER VI

KNOTS

In most books on angling one will find quite a number of knots described for each of the purposes in which they are employed, *i.e.* tying on flies, joining gut, and so on. This practice I do not propose to continue here since it seems to me that if one knows and uses one really good and satisfactory knot for each job, then knowledge of others

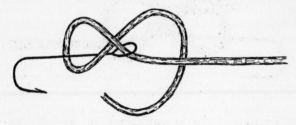

FIG. 1.

is really superfluous. The desiderata for a good knot are that it should (1) not slip, (2) be easily tied and untied, (3) have the free end towards the tail of fly or lure, (4) be neat.

For joining fly to cast all these are contained in the Cairnton knot. The fly is held by the finger and thumb of the left hand close to the head, and an ample length of the gut is passed through the eye, over the first finger, round the hook and in through the loop thus formed (Fig. 1). (Were this pulled tight it would form a simple half-hitch round the shank of the hook, with the free end facing up the cast.) The free end is continued over

the top of the hook, and round and under the cast
which in the meantime has been held gently taut
by the third and fourth fingers of the right hand (the
hook, of course, is in the left hand). There is
now a complete loop and a half, the former round
the hook and the latter round the cast. The latter is
completed by bringing the free end up and through
the half-loop. This free end is continued backwards down the hook and held between the first
finger of the left hand and the hook shank (Fig. 2).
Now the loop round the cast is brought back
over the eye and pulled tight between eye and
head, not, however, with the free end but with
the part leading to the loop first formed. With a

FIG. 2.

little practice this is easily held in position for a
moment while the right hand pulls the cast so that
the rest of the slack is drawn up and the knot
completed.

The points of this knot are that it is neat and
effective, and the end of the gut is so controlled before
any of the knot is pulled tight that it can always
be of exactly the right length. The description,
perhaps almost inevitably, sounds complicated, but
I hope it and the drawings will make the idea
sufficiently plain to be understood.

The Cairnton knot may also be used to join cast
to line. As it happens I always use it when I have
not a link of gut with an eye spliced on to the line.
Some anglers employ for this purpose a simple
half-hitch with a knot on the end of the line to

prevent the end slipping through. In this case the
end is facing up instead of down the line, though
whether this be a serious drawback when heavy gut
is employed in heavy water is perhaps open to
question.

For joining gut nothing equals the well-known
blood knot which is the essence of simplicity and
effectiveness. The two pieces to be joined are
placed parallel, but about an eighth of an inch apart,
between the thumb and forefinger of the left hand,
within thick gut, about an inch and a quarter of gut
clear at the free ends and, if a piece is to be added
to a cast, with the cast towards the right. The
cast is now held taut by locking it between the

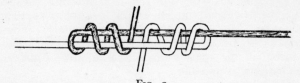

Fig. 3.

third and fourth fingers of the right hand and
exerting a gentle pull. Working from the body
outwards, the first finger and thumb of the right
hand then turn the free end of the gut link two
complete turns round the cast and pass it backwards and downwards through the angle formed
between cast and piece of gut close to the thumb
and finger (Fig. 3). The completed portion, including the turned down end of gut, is now held firm
by the first finger and thumb of the right hand, and
the corresponding procedure of holding and twisting
by the left hand is carried out. In this case the
twist is made in the opposite direction to that made
by the right hand, and the end of gut is passed
through what is now the central loop in a direction
opposite to that of the first end (Fig. 3). If all be
right we now have two twists of gut above and
below a central point, from which project the free

ends in opposite directions at right angles to the general direction of the cast.

The blood knot is drawn up by pulling on the cast and gut link, and, if necessary, gently humouring the turns into position. This last operation is helped if the half-made knot be dipped in water (the gut must previously have been well soaked, preferably in warm water) which acts as a lubricant. Finally the knot should be pulled quite tight before the ends are cut off as close as possible.

Sometimes with very thick gut, when the danger of the knot slipping is increased, three turns instead of two are made in the two parts of the knot.

If a whole cast is being made, I find it convenient to soak the necessary gut, of such different sizes as may be required, make, and if necessary correct, the taper, but only make the knots loosely. Then resoak the whole and pull the knots tight before cutting off the spare ends which should, of course, be as short as possible.

When a cast is to be used with a dropper, the dropper link may most conveniently be part of the cast itself, enough gut being left standing out from one of the knots for the purpose. This dropper end, however, should form part of a link belonging to the cast above, and not below, the knot. Then, if in the course of playing a fish the knot opens, all will be well, and if the trailing tail fly catches in an obstruction and the double pull opens the knot, the fish will be saved and only the tail fly and part of the cast be lost. Such a dropper stands out at right angles to the cast, but should be no longer than sufficient to give sufficient length to tie on the fly : if too long it is apt to wrap round the cast when fishing.

For spinning tackle when joining wire to a swivel, the wire should be passed through the ring and then twisted to the main wire. A pin, small nail, or other similar implement through the wire close to the swivel helps the operation and prevents the knot being drawn too tight. The two wires should be twisted together so that each gradually wraps round the other and not merely so that the free end is wound round the main part which remains straight, although finally the twist may be finished off with two or three turns in this last fashion.

If the trace be of nylon, the best knot is the seaman's anchor knot, which is made by passing the gut twice through the swivel eye in two even turns side by side, and then putting the free end over the main part and under both loops. The end is then at right angles to the trace, and the knot after being pulled tight, may be finished off by making one or two half-hitches, or by putting on a small whipping to hold the end to the main part. When finished the whipping should be varnished. Knots made in nylon are apt to slip, but the anchor knot backed by a half-hitch is quite safe as is the Cairnton with gut for flies.

None of the knots ordinarily used for forming the loop on a cast is really satisfactory. None of them result in the cast leaving the loop knot in a truly central position and the loop is consequently not in line with the cast. This knot also forms the weakest part of the cast ; so much so that with nylon the top strand should always be thicker than the rest of the cast. The only satisfactory knot is a blood knot formed by making the loop of a separate piece of gut or nylon joined to the main part of the cast by a blood knot, one side of which consists of the double strand of the loop. This knot is not easy to draw up tidily and patience may be required to ease the strands into position.

To make a whipping in repairing damage to, or putting a ring on, a rod, in fastening down the ends of gut substitute traces, joining casting line to backing, and so on, a piece of moderately fine silk well rubbed with cobbler's wax, or with one of the waxes which can be made or bought for the purpose, is used. One end of the silk is laid along the subject

in hand, and the other is then laid in turns, each of
which is pulled tight and pushed as close as possible
to its neighbour, over this until within three or
four turns of the desired end. These last turns are
made loose (over a finger laid along the object is
a convenient method) and the end is then passed
back through them towards the commencement
of the whipping. Each turn, starting with that
nearest the last tight turn, is now taken in order,
pulled tight and laid neatly in its place until finally
the whipping is finished, except that a loose loop
is left, and the end is passed backwards under the
last three or four turns. A pull on the free end will
reduce the loop, and it should finally be pulled slowly
tight, at the same time smoothing out any kinks
which may form in the remaining loop. The waste
end is then cut off, the whipping, if necessary, rubbed
down smooth with a small dry, clean bone, a round
pencil, or any other suitable object, and varnished
with spirit varnish or a cellulose preparation.
Waxed silk on a rod should always have one coat
of spirit varnish, for otherwise the copal varnish
put on the whole rod later may not dry at this spot.

If the piece of silk used be short, or other difficulty
arise in making the finish, an auxiliary piece of silk
doubled back to form a loop may be placed under
the final turns, which are drawn tight in the same
manner as the others when they are laid on top of
it. Finally the free end is placed in the loop. The
free ends of the loop which project from among the
turns are then pulled so that the loop and the end
of the whipping silk with it is drawn through the
final turns. At the end of a rod, or in other convenient position, the end of the silk may be laid back
before the final turns are made, and they may
then be laid directly on top of it by passing the
side of the silk forming the turns over the end of
the rod as each round is made.

CHAPTER VII

GREASED LINE FISHING

During the last fifty years we have seen revolu-
tionary changes in many walks of life. In salmon
fishing in particular the revision of thought and
method is as great as in any other sport or in more
prosaic pursuits. Gone are the days of rods twenty
feet long, bought at a shilling per foot. Gone too are
ideas that, once a porter-coloured flood has really
subsided, the chances of sport are poor until rain
or melting snow comes once again to the aid of the
angler. Six or more feet off the length, and nineteen shillings per foot on to the price now accord
with the ideas of modern anglers and tackle-makers.
Once February and March are passed, the porter-
colour flood is accepted chiefly as a means to an end.
It is now regarded as the bearer of a fresh stock of fish
which will provide more and better sport when the
flood is out of the way, than during its progress
and the earlier stages of its decline.

It is difficult to say what may have been the
genesis of this change of view. Certainly the modern
rod-maker and spinner and dresser of lines has
materially contributed to the result by the increased
power combined with lessened weight of the
weapons, be they of split bamboo or, as many
still prefer, of spliced greenheart, and the greater
casting capabilities of the lines. Angling has also
become more of an industry. Inquiring men have
wanted to know the why and the wherefore.
Owners have desired to increase their bags. Tenants
wish to catch as many fish as possible in the comparatively short time available to them. Experiences
have been aired in print and ideas have been

exchanged by this means in a much wider circle and with far greater publicity than was ever common in earlier years. As in other enterprises angling has not been allowed to stand still but, in the modern phrase, has progressed with the times.

It is conceivable that the casual taking of a salmon by a trout angler may have brought the possibilities of light tackle to the fore after the first fine rapture of the apparently miraculous capture had been to some extent dulled by repetition, and by the dampening effect of the well-advertised similar experiences of others. Certain anglers primarily concerned with trout in a well-known trouting river of Scotland sometimes derive almost as much sport from salmon as from trout when the water is so low as to make the professedly exclusive salmon angler believe that attempts for the major fish are only of use in the earlier hours of the day before the sun has developed its full power, or towards evening when it is on its decline and the approaching night hides the grosser details of line, cast, and lure.

The sight of the exciting influence which a hatch of fly may apparently have on kelt and clean salmon alike in the spring cannot fail also to make any thinking angler believe that something of the same size of fly fished in the normal manner of wet flies for trout might possibly be effective. More effective perhaps than is the conventional larger fly fished near the bottom, where both it and its accompaniments are open to only too easy inspection without the necessity for any intimate examination in the mouth of the fish.

The natural fly which seems to rouse the fish from their habitual lethargy on or near the bottom of the river may be many kinds. ' March browns,' within which category may apparently be included many different flies of somewhat similar appearance, are perhaps the most common, though the appearance of other flies in sufficient numbers may also coincide with a similar display of desirable activity. No one, however, has yet so far as I am aware attempted to work out the true relationship between the observed facts. It may be that the fly excites the salmon, but on the other hand it is also possible that the conditions and temperature of water and atmosphere which conduce to a good hatch of fly also stir up the salmon.

Too many people have been misled by the relationship of apparent cause with effect for us to take, without some proof of a much more definite kind, the presumed connection between fly and fish as a definite fact. Indeed it would almost seem that the connection is more apparent than real. Salmon will certainly ' head and tail,' their action during a hatch of fly, when there is no fly about. We all know the typical rise ' to himself,' in the ghillie's phrase, of a ' taking ' fish. Salmon will also very frequently ' head and tail ' when they are running, and just after entering a pool, more especially if they have had to face some rough or fast water before gaining the sanctuary of the quieter area. One can frequently see them when the river is low in the clear water of the tidal pools where no fly exists rising head and tail freely during the last of the ebb and as the flood tide first commences to flow but before the latter has gained sufficient impetus to disturb them and urge their ascent to the next higher pool. Though it is quite possible, when the tide and other conditions are right, to catch salmon in such pools under most conditions, they will certainly take much more freely when they are in the mood which produces the frequent head and tail rise without the stimulus of natural or artificial fly. Salmon may also be seen at times rising head and tail in the sea, in purely salt water, but here more frequently they demonstrate their presence by a jump into the air. One may also see them very frequently ' heading and tailing ' at the side of the stream where a river

6

enters straight into the sea without the intervention of any real tidal pool in the accepted sense of the term.

Various attempts have been made, notably by the late Major Fraser, to translate the observed fact of the apparent rise to the natural fly into appropriate action for the benefit of the angler, but without any material success in Great Britain. This might be taken to indicate the lack of connection between the free rise of the fish and a hatch of natural fly. On the other hand, a salmon will take a floating fly in the gin-clear rivers in Newfoundland and the eastern side of Canada where the fish can be seen and the fly dropped immediately above their noses. In our less clear and less thickly inhabited waters, where such precision is not normally possible, they are apt to dispute man's interpretation of their behaviour by ignoring the substitute fly. But the half-way house of the imitation insect just submerged proves much more to their liking.

The late Mr. A. H. E. Wood of Glassel has told in his own words the beginning of this idea and its subsequent development, and it is not now necessary for me to do other than repeat in merest outline the essential facts. In a river in Ireland he saw salmon rising during a hatch of white moths when ordinary methods of angling did not produce results commensurate with those which apparently might be expected. Then, seated on the bridge of an eel weir, he dropped an artificial fly and observed the behaviour of both it and the fish, and the response necessary for success from the angler. The primary idea developed and the first facts ascertained, the subsequent refinements have been the result of time, thought, and orderly experiment.

An important point was also brought out by Mr. Wood when he first tempted the fish from that bridge at the Irish eel weir. Salmon not only rise slowly, but they also eject any object from their mouth slowly.

A trout, active and lively, seizes its prey with avidity, bites hard, and possibly chews it. If the object be not what is expected, the reaction is immediate in its violence. A salmon on the other hand will roll even a hard and prickly object, such as an artificial fly, round its tongue. Unless strain be applied, it apparently for a time finds nothing uncommon or alarming in the mixture of steel and feathers.

Here then are the facts on which this particular method of fishing which we are at present considering is based. Salmon rise slowly and, given the opportunity, are equally slow to reject any object which takes their fancy. Finally, experience and observation have shown that under certain conditions salmon will take a fly more readily when it is swimming near the surface than when it is either in mid-water or as near the bottom as circumstances will allow. Mid-water appears to be the worst position of all : in really cold water as near the fish as possible is best. In April and May the sub-surface fly will beat the other practically every time, but for its success the atmosphere must be warmer than the water.

Let us take first the problem of keeping the fly near the surface. In still or very quiet water this can be done by moving the rod point or pulling the line in through the rings with sufficient speed, and yet at the same time without moving the fly unduly quickly. In fast water such a manœuvre is not possible without the development of excessive speed. In either position, however, the desired result can be achieved much more easily by adopting the dry fly fisherman's habit of greasing the line. This proceeding has two advantages. It keeps the cast and fly near the surface, and it gives the angler a great deal of control over the movement of line and lure.

The cast and fly, on the other hand, should never be greased, and the reason for this will speedily be seen if the cast picks up grease by accidental contact with rod or line. Every knot then has, when drawn along the water surface, its own wake. The whole cast is flanked by a succession of miniature waves on each side all the way from fly to line. I have known of one angler who defied convention in this matter, and in so doing increased the bag obtained by sunk fly by many times its former total. But the general effect is so displeasing that I have never heard of an imitator. In fact, if the line has been greased a little too far, the knot joining line to cast may refuse to sink and create its own bow wave. The last foot or so of the line should never be greased, but any difficulty on this score can be avoided by splicing the single length of treble gut with a loop on one end, to which reference has been previously made, to the line. The cast is then rove through the loop, and so long as the cast itself does not float, all is well.

If grease gets on to the cast or it is desired to sink the line for ordinary fishing, they should be rubbed with a handful of grass or leaves of the dock plant. Clay rubbed on also helps to keep everything that is necessary below the surface.

The old-fashioned ghillie's idea of a well-cast line was one at an angle of 45 degrees downstream with rod, line, cast, and fly as straight as a bar. Short rises, ' plucks,' and similar phenomena were then a feature of every suitable angling day. The typical and normally most useful cast when fishing with a greased line is at, or nearly at, right angles to the line of the river, with plenty of slack lying on the surface as well as in the angler's hand. Such casting would be stigmatized in various uncomplimentary fashions by anglers of the older school. Its object, however, is threefold. It first of all allows the fly to drift down with the stream, bobbing in and out of the varying currents and eddies with no more than a minimum amount of pull from the cast and line. Thus the fly resembles some object coming down naturally with the current. It turns and twists. The feathers of wing and hackle have a chance of working which is denied to them when swinging round at the end of a taut line. 'Flash' from topping or tail, from ribbing or body, has the greatest opportunity of making its appeal as the fly pitches or rolls on an even keel. The slack also allows a fish to take the fly and return towards, if not actually to, the bottom without feeling any resistance to its progress. Finally, paradoxical as it may seem, the slack allows the angler to control the position and movement of the fly with considerable accuracy, and without disturbing the even movement of the lure.

In ordinary sunk line fishing variable control of the lure can be exercised to only a slight degree. A switch over of the line immediately after the cast is made, and a similar but even less effective manœuvre elsewhere in the arc of travel, are about all that can be done.

On the other hand, with a greased and floating line the fly is under the almost immediate control of the angler from the time it alights upon the water until it is lifted for the next cast.

This control may take several forms. The most obvious is the simple switch upstream, just as in sunk line fishing, to prevent a belly in the line which would drag the fly across the stream practically out of control. But unlike sunk line fishing, the switching may be continued indefinitely, and in this way the fly may be kept out in the stream and brought in to the bank as slowly as the angler desires. In addition, its line of travel may be controlled so as to bring it through any particular ripple or past any definite lie in the most attractive fashion, whatever may be the position of the lie or the strength of the stream.

It is also sometimes useful and profitable to fish down the edge of a stream of stronger water. A further very pretty and effective method is to cast across a strong stream into slack water beyond. In this last case a succession of short quick switches upstream brings the fly through the slack water with a sink and draw motion which sometimes proves to be most attractive to the fish. Finally, should the fly be travelling too slowly, a switch in the down-stream direction will put a curve on the line on which the current may act to increase the speed of travel of the lure.

The actual movement which effects the switch-over of the line is simple. Its successful application is not quite so easy. The beginner even with plenty of slack line on the surface will inevitably move rod and line too violently, and the fly will jump a few inches or even a few feet in the water. The sight of one or two fish rising to the fly just when this move occurs provides a most effective check to the practice. In making the move, the rod point should travel smoothly through an even arc, and sufficient of the slack line held in the unoccupied hand should be yielded to act as a buffer spring which prevents movement in the line on the water beyond the point to which it is desired to lift it. As in so many other delicate operations, the description in detail is difficult, and only practice, once the essential principle is mastered, can produce perfection.

A few words, perhaps, are necessary on the mode of attack when a fish does rise to the fly. In this method of fishing in clear water with the lure at the surface, one sees a great deal more of the movements of the fish than in any other kind of angling, except perhaps dry fly fishing for trout. This clear view of the fish adds vastly to one's pleasure. The fish appear to come to the fly astonishingly slowly, and to take it with the gravest deliberation. In a competition to move the fly

first the angler can easily win every time, and
the temptation to do so has undoubtedly saved the
lives of many fish. All thoughts of striking on the
rise must be definitely abandoned, and no more
must be made until the fish is felt or is at least far
on its way back to the bottom. Then with the
larger sizes of hooks used in this method—numbers
1 to 4 or $1\frac{1}{4}$ inches to 1 inch in length—only a
gentle strike is required, and with smaller hooks
a mere tightening of the line is sufficient.

If the current be at all strong it will have carried
the slack of the line downstream of the fish before
the latter is hooked, and the hook will then pene-
trate the best holding position at the corner of the
mouth, and not merely hit hard bone or loose
skin elsewhere. I know of no more interesting
moment in fishing than to see the rise and descent
of a good fish, and then to raise the rod point to
see if it has made a good shot or thought better
of it at the last moment. If, after the cast was
made, the fly has drifted down 35 to 40 yards,
as may easily be done by paying out line, the interest
and uncertainty are greatly increased. Short rises
are as often due to a cast which is too thick as to a
fly which is too large, or which for its size is moving
too slowly.

Any kind of rod may be used for greased line
fishing, and most people prefer a double-handed
weapon of thirteen or fourteen feet for ease of
casting. Mr. Wood employed twelve-feet rods of
varying strengths and used them single-handed,
but this is scarcely possible for those not gifted
with his strength of arm. Personally, I find a rod
of that length necessary for the larger flies of the
sizes mentioned above. I, however, prefer a rather
lighter one of eleven feet six inches for the smaller
flies, from number 4 to number 10 (1 inch to $\frac{5}{8}$ inch)
or even smaller. I find that the use of one hand for
the rod and the other to hold and release the slack
line renders switching over easy and the control of

line and fly more accurate. With small flies and
light casts the rod also must be in proportion, and
one certainly gets far better sport from such tackle
than from the heavier, and what is usually regarded
as the more typical, salmon gear.

Chapter VIII

SPRING FISHING

Spring fishing differs from every other form of
fly fishing. The object of the angler at that time
is to get the fly to travel as slowly and as deep as
possible. It is a time when the largest flies are of
use, and would-be critics are apt to be somewhat
scornful of the whole business.

There is, however, something very attractive
about this branch of the sport. It is a man's job.
The size, or rather the type, of rod and line must
match the fly, and more often than not one has
to war against the elements as well as against the
fish. Snow, sleet, and a gale of wind are no uncommon events in January and February. A calm
day is the exception, and then frost with ice on
line and rings is often an accompaniment of the
start and finish of each day.

Ice is perhaps one of the worst enemies of the
spring fisher, whether it appears on the water surface
or in the rod rings. Unless unusually bad, however,
it may be adequately dealt with in both places, and
on a cold, frosty morning a little exercise in pushing
ice off the sides of the pools with the aid of a long
and strong pole having a bifurcated end between
the points of which is stretched a few strands of
wire is no bad tonic for starting the circulation,
and warming one up. But that evil cousin, sub-
surface and slushy, of ice called ' grue ' is a creature
of quite another calibre, by which one has invariably
to admit defeat. No fly, bait, or line can compete with
its tenacity and floating properties, and when it is
present in any quantity, nothing remains but to leave
the rod in its place of rest until conditions improve.

When ice free, the rivers too flow black and full. Where later one will stand when fishing in May or June, several feet of water flow, and all indication of the lies on which one will then rely is lost in the general turmoil of the stream.

Spring fishing is also a matter of contrasts. At one pool the bank may be iron hard with the whiteness of last night's frost still on the surface. The shadow cast by the neighbouring trees makes one glad of some protection for the hands, and the breeze coming up the strath has an almost too penetrating chill. At the next pool, lower down and round the corner, the plantation on the north-east keeps off the wind, the high sloping bank gathers in the warmth of the sun, and one is tempted to linger, smoking a pipe or pretending to look for the first sign of spring growth.

So long as winter conditions remain and the water temperature is definitely below 40° F., salmon behave in a manner clearly distinguished from their habits later in the year when the water is warmer. During cold weather, they seek and keep to the deeper and slower pools. When on the move they avoid, so far as is possible, the streams and rapids, and altogether decline to face any obstruction of even a minor character, which later they will tackle and overcome with ease. They travel slowly and almost exclusively in daylight, except perhaps when they make passage into fresh water with the aid of the tide.

Not only do the fish travel slowly, but they also move slowly to the fly, and their interest can be stirred only equally slowly. Until about the end of March, more can often be taken by spinning than by fly fishing, but in some waters spinning is not permitted, and certain anglers still also prefer to stick to the fly in spite of the bigger bags which might be obtained by other means.

One of the secrets of success in spinning is probably that the lure gets right down to the bottom, and can be worked so that it travels slowly. In spinning at that season one wants to feel the lead and lure almost scraping along the bottom. Fish one ever so wisely or well, it is sometimes quite impossible to get a fly anywhere near the bottom, owing either to the depth of water and position from which one must cast or by reason of the run of the currents.

The head waters of a pool are scarcely ever of any use in the early spring, although if there be a moderately deep, quiet pool, even of very small size, alongside the stream, it is worth a cast, especially during the middle of a relatively warm day. Fish may be then on the move, and it is possible to pick up one waiting in such a lie before essaying to make its passage among the eddies and in slack water behind the stones on the way to the pool above.

The best of the water is usually the lower middle section of each pool, and especially if there be a rocky point or obstruction extending out into the stream and creating an area of slack water of sufficient depth below. A croy or a little subsidiary building on some natural features may often improve the holding capacity of this part of a pool for spring fish. They will not lie in strong water, wherever it be, and if, of the two sides of a pool, one is slacker than the other they will choose the former. The water may continue to be good down towards the tail, but as soon as it begins to gather speed for the exit, fishing may be stopped. Sometimes, however, one finds fish lying in surprisingly thin water near the tail if they have good lies and the pool itself be definitely slack or dead and the glide gentle.

In casting the large spring flies, one must give them a good start in the backward lift, in order to get them well into the air, and then allow plenty of time for the line to get to its full extent before the forward movement of the rod is begun. The casts should be made definitely in a downstream direction quite the reverse of the later fishing, and at an angle as acute as will allow the whole of the available water to be covered. If the current exert any pull, the line should be switched over several times so as to reduce the speed of travel to a minimum. If it be possible to allow everything to go quite slack directly after the fly has alighted in the water so much the better, as this provides a chance for it to be well sunk right from the time it starts to fish.

Any stone, depression in the bottom, or other break in suitable water provides a possible lie for a spring fish, but they seem to prefer above all to lie just at the side junction of a stream and slack water. In one river in the north of Scotland the water held up by a cruive dyke comes through the old cruive box openings with the strength of a mill stream, and on each side of this forceful exit is water deep, black, and still, headed by the dyke and extending down to where the cruive streams break and spread into the large pool below. Until the water below rises, the streams are too strong for spring fish, but they edge up and lie close in to the stream just below the boxes. Lies of the right type and sufficient size are an invaluable asset in such positions.

The most effective way of catching these fish is not that which would appear to be the most simple, that is, to cast right into the slack water. It is probable that in spite of the smooth surface various currents and eddies are at work underneath, and that the fly does not ' work ' properly but goes about in an uneven and unattractive manner. The effective method is to cast the fly into the stream and let it swing round into the slack, doing at the same time what is possible to keep it deep. Fish will be found to take just as the fly leaves the strong water, and if it be possible to stand so that the rod point is directly in line with the junction, fishing will be rendered better and easier.

If one has to cast across a stream which is not too strong into dead water beyond, one method of arousing the fish's curiosity is to adopt a definite ' sink and draw ' motion instead of letting the fly be drawn slowly off by the action of the current on the line. Merely vibrating the rod point will not achieve the result intended : the rod must be lifted to an angle of about 45° (the exact amount varies with length of line out, strength of current, and so on), and then dropped suddenly. The same result can be brought about by continually and rather violently switching over a floating line.

When the water is reasonably clear, it is always worth while to take out a rod equipped with a greased line and a fly size 1 (1¼ inch) as well as the heavier weapon. For an hour or so fish may come to the smaller fly, which, fished slowly, will sink somewhat in spite of the floating line. Especially should one try in the shallower water and towards the tail of the pool if fish be lying in the glide. One sometimes may get them also in dead water by pulling the line in slowly through the rings. If one be fishing a small fish river, the method is well worth a trial, by reason of the better sport which fish of under ten or twelve pounds give on the lighter rod and tackle. An essential requirement, however, before even attempting floating line fishing, is that, whatever the water temperature, the air should be at least several degrees warmer than the water.

As the water becomes warmer, so have the methods of the spring anglers to be changed until by May a radical alteration is completed, and fishing then resembles that of summer.

In Scotland, in normal years, the latter half of March and the first half of April is often a most unsatisfactory time for the angler. The weather and water are beginning to warm up, but conditions change so radically from day to day that while to-day may resemble summer, to-morrow may be back into midwinter. The angler does not know whether to put on or take off extra clothing. The fish do not know whether to stay where they are or move into the stream, nor is the size of fly which will tickle their fancy at all certain. One has to be prepared not only against the weather but also with a varying assortment of cast and fly sizes in order to find that which may be most effective for the day, or even part of the day. Angling at that time is an uphill business, and only by keeping a continual check on the water and air temperatures, and varying not only the lures but also the exact parts of the pools which are fished, can the angler hope to achieve any great measure of success.

When fishing a sunk fly at that time, the range of sizes may be as great as from $4/0\frac{1}{4}$ (2 inch) in the morning, down to a 1/0 or even a number 1 at lunch time, and then back to perhaps $5/0\frac{1}{2}$ just as dusk turns to darkness. The cast should be changed at least once and possibly twice to match the change in size of fly. With a greased line a fly as small as a number 4 (1 inch) may be useful.

In the latter part of April in Scotland, and earlier in England, a definite climatic change occurs. None of the nights are as cold as earlier in the year, and most are relatively mild : the days are much longer, and the sun has a considerably greater chance of warming up the water. Temperatures of under $40°$ F. cease to appear in the water records, and everything becomes quite clearly spring instead of winter. The proprietors of the lowest waters in the larger rivers find their season ebbing or gone. The fresh fish may run through not only the tide but also several miles of fresh water without a halt, or with only a minimum amount of rest. They pass by on their way many of the earlier fish still faithful to their first choice of lie, where indeed some of them may remain throughout most of the summer.

Later some, but a very small proportion, of those which have gone on upstream, will come back and may be found even in tidal waters or caught out in the nets set on the open sea coast. Known most appropriately as ' droppers,' their exact history and the reason for the retrograde movement are obscure. So far as has been ascertained, their development is normal, and nothing to cause the difference in habit from the vast majority of their fellows is apparent.

With the climatic change comes the concomitant change in the habits of the fish. Only the kelts and the very stale fish remain in the slack water, and the fresh and taking fish are to be found in the faster water of the body of the pool and in the more rapid glide of the tail. They are not as yet in the very rapid streams like the grilse, but they have a definite preference for the stronger waters.

They will now take a fly more readily than a minnow at all times. The cast must be finer, and the lure must be considerably smaller and fished faster than has been the case up to this date. Flies between number 1 and number 6 ($1\frac{1}{4}$ to $\frac{3}{4}$ inch) in ordinary water are most appropriate, and casting should be more square across rather than downstream. Many of the methods described in the chapter on grilse fishing may be employed, and the finer one fishes in reason the greater will be the bag.

But for this later fishing, which in many middle beats is really the cream of the spring fishing, I much prefer the greased line to any other method. It probably yields more fish, it provides more interesting fishing, and it certainly is altogether more amusing than when one uses a sunk line and fly, and normally knows nothing until the pull of a fish is felt.

Chapter IX

SPRING FISHING IN LOW WATER

We are accustomed to associate spring salmon fishing with cold weather and high water. So long as weather and wind be not too cold or the water over high, it is what we welcome and pray for. All will agree, I am sure, that such conditions approach as nearly as possible to the ideal when the places where fish may be found are fairly well defined. We may then heave out our well-tried lures, be they fly or minnow, with a feeling of certainty that if the fish are there some surely will be on the take, and sport may be anticipated with at least a reasonable spirit of optimism. If nature be over-generous, we may still look in quiet corners and the slacker water off the main stream for the fish which are surely taking shelter from the wilder current of mid-river, and from those places where, concentrated by the outline of the bank and the configuration of the bottom, it rips and roars in the course of its passage to the sea. Provided the water is not thickened too much by suspended matter and general débris, there is always hope of a fish, and possibly of rather more than usual excitement before it is brought to the gaff.

Occasionally, however, we are faced with a situation which is by no means easily handled.

In a normal winter, rivers in the north at all events only fall to a low level when much frost is present and when consequently the reduced waters are much encumbered with ice and grue, if indeed they are not completely covered with a uniform white sheet. On other comparatively rare occasions, however, we may find exceedingly low

rivers combined with mild weather and no ice.
No physical difficulty against fishing then presents
itself, and except for the paucity of water there is
no apparent reason why fish should not be caught
in steady if somewhat limited numbers, provided
one can only find the right type of lure and appropriate method of its use.

In February and March one may sometimes be
without a fish although plenty are in the water
and the latter is at a level which would provide
at least moderately good sport a couple of
months later, when the temperature has risen
considerably.

In the comparison of the temperatures, we may
perhaps find the basic reason for the difference in the
value of the sport obtained at the same water
heights. However low the water may be when the
temperature is only from 34° to 38° F. the fish
persist in lying in the quieter places, and if not in the
eddies, certainly in the slack current, where everything is only too obviously clear to them. They
are also lethargic, difficult to interest, and slow to
move, so that they easily see not only too much of
what occurs on the bank but also too much of the
fly or other lure in the water. Either their curiosity
is satisfied without the necessity of making the
decisive grasp, or if the lure be fished fast enough
to prevent this they simply cannot be troubled to
hunt after and catch it before it has disappeared for
good. Later when the water is several degrees
above the critical limit and only occasionally at
night falls to, or slightly below, 40° F., the fish
lie in stronger water, where the details of fly, cast,
and line are less visible. They are also then far
more energetic, the lure can be worked faster, and
they will certainly make much greater efforts to
secure it, although if fished too slowly they may still
see too much and decide to let evil alone. When
trying to catch salmon in low water in February and
March, we are therefore apparently attempting the

7

impossible. But like most other difficulties, this can be to some extent at least surmounted, and at times one may obtain some reward for one's effort.

I think that perhaps the first point to be borne in mind is that in the circumstances postulated a relatively considerable change may occur in the temperature of the water during the day, and that the effect of the angle of sun and light will certainly vary materially from dawn until dusk. In consequence, the size of lure will, on the basis of the colder the water the larger the lure necessary, vary from hour to hour, and the chances of readily deceiving the fish will be greater during the earlier morning and later evening when the sun is low or possibly below the horizon altogether, than during high noon and the interval immediately preceding and succeeding that period.

It is possible that many anglers, willing enough in the event of non-success to change the pattern of fly at their own or the ghillie's suggestion, are always too loth to change the size as the conditions vary from pool to pool, or indeed in some cases in different parts of the same pool. It is certain that if, again, in the circumstances with which we are at present dealing, no change of size of fly or other lure is made throughout the day, then we are definitely giving ourselves less chance of catching fish than would be the case were we more enterprising, and did we consider more carefully the exact facts with which we have to deal.

In the early morning, and before breakfast, will sometimes be none too early to start, when the chill is still in the air, and the first rays of the sun are only just reaching the water, if indeed they reach it at all, the larger sizes will be both admissible and effective. A fly of two and a half inches with its proper weight of cast will not be out of place, and a spinning bait even slightly larger may be tried.

Rapidly, however, as the sun ascends and more especially if the water be not deep, or a move made to shallower reaches, the size used will have to be reduced to flies or minnows of two inches and one and a half inches in length, with a less stout cast or trace to suit the smaller strain involved. These may be fished slightly faster, but not a great deal more rapidly, or the fish will not bother about them. If the ghillie can be stationed where observation is possible and fish are seen to follow the lure, then it is moderately certain that it is too big or the cast too thick. In the middle of the day, a fly an inch long or slightly less, or a small natural minnow or phantom may be large enough, but as evening approaches the process has to be reversed.

At the fall of darkness, perhaps the most deadly time of the whole day, and for which it may be advisable to leave a bit of the best of the water undisturbed, the fly may be as large and the cast as strong as were those used at the start. It may also be as well to fish rather later than is customary : to stop only some time after it has been found possible to see the fly or minnow alight on the water, may at times prove to be not unprofitable.

If the temperature of the air be markedly higher than that of the water for a time in the middle of the day, a greased line and a fly of between half an inch and an inch length may be quite successful. I think I am correct in saying that under these conditions this method is definitely more effective, so far as kelts are concerned, than a sunk fly, and it also most probably takes more clean fish. It is certainly a very much more entertaining method of fishing, and even if with the slow movement of the springer and the lack of sign of movement on the surface the angler does not see a great deal more of what goes on underneath the water, the ghillie may very easily obtain a vantage point from which the movement of the fish upwards becomes clear, and from which he may report the success attending

the use of different sizes of flies and the adoption
of varying methods of attack.

Spring salmon fishing in low water is not an easy
business, but has many attractions, and only by the
use of thought and the careful application of primary
principles can any success at all be gained.

Chapter X

GRILSE FISHING

Grilse are attractive little creatures. Full of lithe grace and the activity of youth, they are dashing and energetic. Whether pursuing their way upstream, undaunted by low water or formidable obstacles, or fighting for their life after having taken the angler's lure in mistake for something less deadly, they never know defeat until their last gasp. Only the other day one beaten in battle by me, in spite of leaps and runs worthier of much larger and stronger fish, and actually with its nose out of the water, when being towed on its side up a gravel bank suddenly got rid of the fly and was on an even keel, round and out into deep water in less time than is required to write these few words.

I can imagine nothing more attractive or more entertaining than grilse fishing under pleasant conditions, when the water sparkles and an occasional fish shows here and there in the sunlight or the passing shadow.

Grilse are to be found in our rivers as early as May ; an odd fish may be taken in the nets of the east coast of Scotland in April, or even at the end of March. But it is June before any quantity appear, and July, August, and September are the months when anglers may set forth most hopefully in search of them. They are probably earliest on the middle and upper sections of the east coast of Scotland, and latest on the north-west coast of that country. The west of Scotland and its islands, the south-west of England, and the west of Ireland are the great grilse angling areas : very considerable quantities are also netted in the east of Scotland, the north of Ireland, and the extreme north-east of England.

Great variations occur in their numbers. The high-water mark was probably reached in 1895, but from then until 1908 or 1910 the grilse crop in most districts remained at a good level. From 1910 onwards a decline to a very low figure was rapid, and only within the last fifteen years has any recovery been shown. Notable exceptions to the general conditions, however, exist and more particularly in some of the smaller districts where neither fresh nor salt water nets are worked or, if present, are only used in the sea some distance from the river mouth.

Grilse, especially when fresh run, are very tender mouthed, and they are found at the time of year when the light is strong and waters are usually below their average level. The tackle therefore must be fine, the rod supple rather than stiff, and the handling, after a fish has been hooked, gentle.

The ideal rod should be between ten and twelve feet in length, decidedly not stiff, and in fact rather whippy, provided it will cast the necessary line with comfort. At times, a longish rod will be rendered more suitable if a top somewhat lighter than the normal can be fitted without destroying the action. As always, the line should exactly match the rod, but if the weapon be right the line will necessarily be light. Except during a very occasional flood or late in the season when conditions generally are more autumnal, small flies during the day time will be necessary, and the cast must therefore be fine. To gain the greatest help in throwing the fly, and to ensure general lightness, the cast must be tapered evenly throughout from a thickness which matches the link attached to the line at the top to that appropriate to water and fly at the other end. Everything is also so clearly visible that a cast fourteen, instead of the usual nine, feet long is of material assistance in deceiving the fish, especially in still water. Although tapered casts of nine feet can be purchased, or those of fourteen feet can be specially ordered, the angler in this case, who makes up his own casts, will be at an advantage, since he can make it not only of exactly the desired length to suit any particular conditions but also can pick his gut so that the taper is even and uniform from end to end, whatever may be the thickness of the line or length of cast.

Grilse are generally to be sought in the streams and rougher water, where they make a dash at the fly and are exceedingly quick in turning on it—far more so than adult salmon. One is fishing with a small fly and fine gut, the fish are tender mouthed, and consequently if they take on a tight line nothing more than a pull or, worse still, the loss of the fly commonly results. Precautions should be taken to prevent the fly being dragged across too quickly. If the water be comparatively narrow, this can be done by casting at a more acute angle than usual downstream, or by ' switching over ' so as to take the ' belly ' out of the line. Extra care is also necessary in holding the rod point well up in the air, so that its flexibility may be brought into action immediately a fish touches the fly, and so that there may also be some available slack in the curve of the line between rod point and the place where it enters the water.

In the streams, whatever the angler may do, the fly inevitably comes across the water fairly quickly, and, being small, may not be seen or not seen sufficiently by the fish. It is advisable, therefore, to test the chief known lies by a number of casts, varied a little as to position and angle, before passing on downwards. An alteration of fly from silver to dark body and vice versa may also sometimes be effective, and of course the usual changes may be rung on the sizes called into use.

Grilse are sometimes also found in comparatively slack water, more especially in the smaller rivers. Here the streams are often so shallow and so short as to provide practically no shelter, and the grilse have to occupy the pools where the current, except for a yard or two at the top, is exceedingly gentle. The fisher then has much greater scope for exercising both his skill in casting and his knowledge of the finesse of fishing. Too often, owing to lack of this skill and knowledge, or of tackle appropriate to the occasion, one will hear such water described as useless or hopeless, although it be well populated with fish.

Unless the water be unruffled by wind, or the noonday sky unflecked by cloud, no reason exists for despair if the right gear and methods be used. The fly must not be too big or the cast at the end too thick, and casting must certainly be so light that the line alights on the water with no more than a ripple to mark its descent. Now, too, the fourteen feet of cast to keep the line well away from the fly will be appreciated.

But correct gear and light casting are not everything. Left to itself, or even when the line is ' switched down ' to put on drag, the fly will only sink deeper and deeper into the water, and will very slowly work its passage round, if indeed it does not find the bottom before the journey is completed. Such fishing is quite unattractive, and resource has to be made to the device of drawing the line in through the rings as described in an earlier chapter.

In this manœuvre almost infinite variety is open to the thinking fisherman, fond of experiment and observant of the reactions of the fish.

The rod point may be held low so that the fly is comparatively deep, and the line brought in either rather slowly or fairly rapidly. In either case danger is to be apprehended from the position of the rod. When a fish takes, there is practically a straight pull between the angler's hand and the fly, and unless great care is taken the parting will be immediate, more especially if only a short line be out with consequently little elasticity.

But such fishing should not be carried on frequently, or for any length of time. Grilse, when fresh run, are not only free risers but come more freely to a fly fished near the surface than to one well down in the water. The same variations of speed may therefore be tried with the rod point held well up, so that line and cast are near the surface, and now, of course, plenty of spring exists to take the first shock of the pull of the fish. In fact, the angler has only to remain quite still and allow the fish to hook itself by its own weight as it goes down.

The fly may also be cast directly across or even slightly upstream, and at any angle downstream. Casting downstream at an acute angle, however, will not usually be found to be very successful.

In fishing in a stream, the fly is brought round by the current, so that, provided no undue distance intervenes between successive casts, the fly and gut are inevitably seen by the fish before the line. In fishing in rather still water, however, when the line is drawn through the rings the fly and gut follow more or less the path of the line. Consequently, except for the part corresponding to the length of the gut cast, the fish see first the line, then the gut, and last of all the lure. The water is also generally clear, and no need exists for explaining or emphasizing the desirability of using a cast as long as may be convenient. In fact, under such circumstances one has always the best chance of getting a fish early in the cast, unless one can induce a rather shy grilse which has been following the fly to take it right at the end, by altering the progress of the fly to a smooth movement, a series of short jerks, a quicker dart and then a stop, or any other form of temptation of which each individual angler can think for himself.

If a particular lie be fished over consciously, it is clearly better to start by allowing the fly to drop just at the desired spot, so that the line is not visible to the fish. Only after several attempts have been made in this fashion without result should a cast beyond the best lie be made.

When one starts to fish on what promises to be a not very favourable day, there is a great temptation to continue in spite of the conditions. When, however, one is fishing for grilse in slack water, and the inimical factor is either lack of wind or too much sun, it is better far to hold one's hand and not fish until the light begins to fade in the evening ; even then, the start should be over delayed rather than made too early. If one fishes while the sun is too high, the wind too soft, or the light too strong, one has an exceedingly poor chance of getting a fish, and almost the certainty of disturbing or scaring them so that they will not take in the evening. Grilse sometimes take well after a hot day at just about the hour when it is time to start sea trout fishing. Usually they go down after dusk, but under certain conditions of temperature or weather they will take like sea trout when it is completely dark.

I remember one night on the upper part of a Ross-shire river particularly well. Firstly, because the midges before dusk were as active as only those in the north-west of Scotland can be—even knee-boots, a veil, and button sleeves failed to be entirely proof against their attacks. Secondly, because for the river I had an excellent bag of sea trout. And thirdly, because in the course of fishing in the dark I actually hooked three salmon. The pool was not very large : heather girt, with a high bank on the south side ; and away to the west the rugged sharp outline of a not inconsiderable peak stood, a clear, sharp, and black silhouette against the still faintly glowing sky, reminiscent of the sunset so lately gone. A slight wind from the south-west had died away and the night was calm, warm, and still. The sea trout had moved into the thinnest of this water at the head and tail of the pool, and the salmon were not far from them. The first fish, probably a grilse, I played for some time : a dull business up and down the pool in which I could do little and the fish no more. Ultimately I thought I would get it, but when drawing it to the beach the dropper fly caught on a rock and the cast parted. With the other two, as soon as I was certain of their species (no big sea trout exist in that river), I simply put the rod point down and pulled : catching sea trout was far greater fun than walking up and down with those creatures, which cruised without energy or enthusiasm, and with which it was difficult to deal effectively in the darkness and with the tackle then employed.

In fine bright weather, grilse undoubtedly take best in the morning and the evening, and particularly, as I have just stated, in the hour between sunset and dark. Very early in the morning does not seem to be particularly good, possibly because the atmosphere is then somewhat chill, though how a fish realizes the warmth or otherwise of the air I have never been able to understand. The air temperature, however, most certainly has a definite reaction on the behaviour of all salmon. Between six and eight o'clock (summer time) is good, and even on a hot summer day grilse may be hopefully expected if sought in the right places, and with the right tackle between those hours.

CHAPTER XI

FISHING IN TIDAL WATERS

One type of salmon fishing has received little attention, and in consequence much good sport is lost. This is fishing in tidal waters which are commonly reputed to be good for sea trout but quite useless for the larger fish. Angling in such places is usually most successful in the summer when the water is low, but may also be engaged in during the spring with a similar water-level, or indeed at any reasonable state of the river.

A small water flow is obviously the best, since fish are then not inclined to run through without a halt, but after all every fish on its way upstream must pass through the tidal waters, so if there be any inducement to stop, a chance of catching them always exists. In dry weather they come up and drop back with the tide, in running water they pass through without resting ; but in the autumn, whatever the state of the river, they are more apt to linger than earlier in the year.

Pools must naturally exist to give the fish shelter and confidence, and medium-sized and smaller rivers with a length of tidal water are better than the larger rivers. For instance, tidal fishing in the Tay would be a rather hopeless proposition until the autumn fish really begin to hang about instead of going on upstream, and a smaller stream which merely flows between sandy dunes or spreads its waters over a level beach straight into the sea is equally useless. It is better if there be outcrops of rock, biggish boulders, weedy pools.

One of the great attractions of tidal water fishing is that the fish are just out of the sea. Each carries its full complement of sea lice, and unless unduly detained by dry weather will shine and glow and glisten as only a sea caught salmon can. There is also the charm of the unusual. We expect to find shore crabs and other smaller forms of sea life among seaweed, and do not anticipate having to clear it off our fly, or to gaff a salmon among its waving fronds. There is a sense of exhilaration also in the scent of the salt sea and the seaweed drying on the beach, in the sound of the waves breaking on the shore at the mouth of the estuary, and the sight of the cliffs, heather speckled and bespangled with gulls, stretching away out into the northern or western ocean.

Under ideal conditions the tackle used must be fine, and in summer a cast tapered down to a quarter or half-drawn will be none too light : gut of ix size may sometimes serve, when nothing else will deceive a shy and suspicious fish.

I know of one district where salmon are caught in a sea loch with astonishingly large flies and strong casts by fishing into shoals as they cruise round leaping and playing as they go. This fishing, however, is in deep water where commonly a good breeze is blowing. The typical tidal pool is neither large nor deep, often rather sheltered by surrounding rocks from the free play of the wind, so that conditions in the two types of area are altogether different. In the smaller tidal pools, flies of number 6 size are the largest that will ever be required, and those down to numbers 12 and 14 may be effective when everything else fails to attract the fish. In fact, an unexpected capture of salmon or grilse on a small fly, when sea trout are the quarry really sought, may be the first indication of the possibility of developing a salmon fishery in waters where the tide ebbs and flows.

When the river is moderately high, the sea pools may be treated and fished as are any others although, of course, fishing has to be done when the tide is out. At that time the water from the strath or glen or hills is dominant, but fish are normally urgent in their desire to continue their passage. The angler is lucky if he finds one willing to tarry long enough to take an interest in his lure. The best chance will certainly be towards the head of the pool and usually just as the incoming tide begins to raise the water at the foot of that pool.

The prettiest fishing and the most interesting time, however, undoubtedly are offered when the river is low. Then the tidal area is filled by an influx of sea water with each flood tide, diluted only to a small extent with held-up fresh water, and various pools, either quite salt, slightly brackish, or purely fresh, are uncommonly clear. The fish, salmon and perhaps more especially grilse, are desperately anxious to get ahead and, one would think, almost hoping against hope, push on with the flood tide from pool to pool until the tidal limit is reached, when they again retreat before they are left stranded in uncomfortable situations. The likelihood of rain or a strong wind urges them to frenzied activity, and they will then perform feats of energy and behave as at no other time. If high tide happens to correspond with the onset of darkness they may even push on into the non-tidal area though the river may be absolutely low.

The behaviour of a shoal of active grilse running before the tide is a sight which is well worth watching, even if no angling be in prospect and no toll anticipated from them. As the flood tide commences they gather courage and come into the river channel, advancing slowly, spreading out and breaking the surface here with a jump, there with a glancing rush, which merely churns up the foam, and there again is stately progress with their backs awash and the dorsal fin just emerging into the air. As they enter a pool they continue in this fashion to the head. Here for a period they remain, still restless and moving about, but for the time being content not to seek further adventure. As the tide rises and the ford into the next pool becomes less long and steep and thin, a desire for further journeying is shown. They begin to nose upstream. Here and there they seek the channel which gives promise of the easiest passage. Gathered together under the guidance of one or two leaders the shoal essays the attempt. Some are in the deeper runs and others are on the shallow patches where they make the white water fly. They may progress only a few yards or nearly to the top of the run, but almost invariably at the first attempt the leaders will suddenly take fright, turn tail, and the whole shoal will retreat in a flurry of flying water back to the greater depth and security of the pool. Soon however, the rising tide gives more and more water, the run is negotiated, and the same procedure is followed at the next and the next pool until the tide is full.

In the very clear water a cast fourteen feet long should always be used, and methods similar to those recommended for grilse fishing should be employed. Fishing is carried on at about the time of low water. Fish may be caught as the tide ebbs, but the best time is just after the flood tide commences to flow. As they come into each pool both salmon and grilse seem to be comfortable and full of confidence. They have run their course and are prepared to wait until the tide allows them to go farther. For the time being they are not interested in running, and are quite prepared to take an interest in the angler's lure. But once they become restless and are busy trying to get on to the next pool, then it is time to move up and go there too, so as to be ready for them at their next halt.

The period of neap tides, that is, before and after the first and last quarters of the moon, gives one longer opportunities for tidal fishing than do spring tides, which occur at the times of new and full moon. During neap tides the water takes longer to flow and to ebb, and consequently one has longer in each pool before the conditions become impossible for angling.

As the tide recedes the fish do not seem to be so happy and confident. It is as if they felt the tide was ebbing and were anxious lest they be stranded, but sometimes one that has temporarily found a secure resting-place can be induced to take a fly.

A thing to be remembered in all tidal fishing is that, unlike their relatives in fresh water, fish are more or less continually on the move. A pool, and still more a lie which is untenanted, at one time may in a very few minutes hold most desirable occupants and again in a very short time may be entirely out of fishing order. One has therefore to make the most of one's opportunities, to be more than usually observant of the changes which are taking place, and be ready to alter one's position and methods with as little delay as possible. The pool and the stream should be tried thoroughly from various angles and several times over, especially as more and more fish are approaching with the rising tide. Odd fish will also creep up ahead of their fellows and quietly take up a position behind a stone in the run where there is just enough water to cover them comfortably. Such may take a fly sliding past the side, or over the top, of the stone if nothing is done to alarm them. A fish coming down with the ebb may stop in a similar position, and sometimes when the tide has filled far beyond the useful and usual fishing limit a final addition to the bag may be made from behind this sort of stone.

The most amusing part of tidal water fishing to my mind is that in the rather deeper flat pools in the sandy part of the estuary. Here fish may lie throughout the whole of that part of the tide when the water is confined between the inter-tidal banks and is not spread all over the upper flat part of the tidal area. The water, except when the river-level rises, is always brackish, and usually the surface, owing to the lack of current, without a natural ripple.

Fishing without any wind is hopeless, and in moderation the more breeze the better. One will often see fish, when present in such pools, moving in various ways. They either jump, or often lunge across the water very much after the manner of a kelt, or they ' head and tail.' They may be caught at any time when conditions are favourable, but undoubtedly the best sport is to be had and the best bags are made when they are ' head and tailing.'

Naturally the brackish water is extraordinarily clear, and any sand on the bottom seems to add to the effect. Not only must the cast be very fine but only the smallest flies, usually of sizes 12 or 14, are of any use. Even so, while some fish may take readily others are remarkably shy or cautious. They will be seen to follow the fly quite quietly as the line is drawn in through the rings, and all the patience and nerve of the angler will be required to prevent him snatching the fly away from them. When a fish is seen to be following the fly, the angler may vary his methods, slightly increasing and decreasing the speed or length of each movement or continuing in an even motion and so on, but in any case the cast should always be fished out right to the end. Very often the fish will take the fly as it comes into shallow water, or just at the very last moment before it must either turn or be stranded. The rod should be brought right up, so that if necessary the fly can be carried on to the very shore, and it should on no account be lifted until the fish has turned away, that is, if it did not take it before so doing. If unscared, the fish may follow again and again the same or other flies, but if scared by the fly being snatched away preparatory to a new cast it will certainly take no further interest in your lures.

8

For the ordinary tidal pool and stream fishing, any of the ordinary types of flies will do, but for the still deeper pools the small flies dressed in a very ' buzzy ' fashion with plenty of hackle standing well out sometimes seem to do best.

I am told that in some rivers in Norway, grilse are caught in tidal waters by a dry fly. This is rather at variance with dry fly fishing for salmon in this country, but here it has usually, if not always, been tried in the non-tidal part of the river. I have never made the experiment myself in tidal waters, but the attempt would be well worth while, and if successful would certainly add a new interest to what is to my mind one of the most attractive places for salmon fishing.

CHAPTER XII

LOCH FISHING

Loch fishing for salmon is often a rather despised sport, though why this should be so I have never been able to discover. It may not require so much skill either in casting or fishing, but still it has an interest all its own, and undoubtedly the better fisherman will obtain the greatest number of fish.

The equipment required is the same as for any other fishing, but long rods are not necessary. Short stiff weapons for trolling and ordinary fly rods of twelve to fourteen feet in length are all that are necessary. Spinning may, of course, also be tried by those who desire it ; but this method, owing to the danger of hooking the other occupants, is not particularly suited for boat work.

Early spring fishing in a loch is rather dull work as the fish are all caught by trolling a phantom minnow or other lure, and the angler takes little or no part in the proceedings until the fish are actually hooked. Loch Ness and Loch Tay are homes of this sport, and a phantom or golden sprat of between three and four inches in length at the end of a thirty or thirty-five yards of line towed behind the boat is the usual means of capture. Two rods are set, one on each side near the stern at right angles to the boat, with a nail or other check in the gunwale, and a corresponding check for the butt on the floor to hold them in position. A stone or other weight is put on the slack of the line so as to give a good check to drive the hook home when a fish takes. Sufficient elasticity exists in the line and rod to prevent a break, and the stone jumps off when the strike is made.

For those who are sufficiently energetic, a more amusing method is for two friends to take the boat and for the positions of the two to be changed periodically. The forward man is primarily responsible for the control of the boat, and the man aft looks after the rods and plays the fish, assisting in the pulling when he is not otherwise engaged. Positions are changed every half-hour or so, or after a fish is landed. Even one person can troll alone, but it is then easier to put the rod (two are rather much of a handful) in position before starting and coil down the necessary length of line near the stretcher. Then when a fair depth of water has been reached the lure can be put over the side so that it does not foul the trace, and the run out of the line can be controlled by setting one foot on the coils. If it be allowed to run free, the lure will probably reach the bottom before any strain comes on. An anchor is also handy to drop when a fish is hooked. One does not, perhaps, get many fish in this fashion but one gets plenty of exercise and, when a fish is hooked, plenty of fun also. On a windy day it can be a good test of patience and of skill in handling boat and gear.

Loch fishing in the later spring, after April, and in summer is, however, far more amusing as then the fish will rise, sometimes very freely, to the fly.

Salmon in a loch have favourite lies, just as definite as those in a river, and success to some extent depends upon the local knowledge of the angler or his boatman. As in a river, a rocky shore and a hard bottom are the most favoured, though sometimes weed beds where the fish lie in the channels between or at the tail of the waving leaves are also attractive to a smaller number of fish. From five to twelve or fifteen feet is the optimum depth, but occasionally fish are caught in very deep water, and often about the same spots. What these can be doing in from thirty to fifty

or sixty or more feet of water I never can understand, but it is certain they cannot be lying on the
bottom, nor from the fact that they are often taken
in much the same positions is it likely that they are
merely cruising fish.

In a loch the wind has more effect on the fish
than in a river. They have a clear tendency to
come to the lee shore, that is, the shore on to which
the wind is blowing. All do not change with a
change of wind, but sufficient do so to make it well
worth while to give the lee shore first a very
thorough trial when any considerable amount of
water is available.

Calm weather or the ordinary good trout fishing
breeze is of little use for salmon fishing, for which
the more wind the better, provided one can remain
afloat. Consequently when fishing fly it is more
convenient to have only one angler, and not two
anglers, in the boat. Under the best conditions the
boat will drift too fast when left broadside on and
should be held rather strongly bow on into the
wind. It is, of course, possible to fish broadside
by putting a big stone over to drag on the bottom,
or a sea-anchor (a large cone of canvas on a wood
or metal ring with both the large and the small
ends open) over the weather side, or by partially
holding the boat up with the oars, so that the bow
rod can fish with difficulty, but none of these
methods is convenient in a really strong wind.

The fishing itself is carried out in a manner
very like that of trout fishing and may be similarly
varied. The flies (one dropper is commonly
employed) may be dabbled on the surface (sometimes this is effective when the wind is rather light),
and they may be cast either down-wind or across
the wave. Long casting is not required, as salmon
are not more shy of a boat than are trout, and I
have repeatedly seen a fly taken practically at the
end of the oar. I even remember a lady once making
desperate, if furtive, efforts to release her fly from,

as she thought, the bottom of the boat without being observed by her fishing partner, whereas she was really fast into a twenty-two pounds fish !

Salmon in a loch seem to me to fall into two classes. The first are the early fish which gradually become scattered all over the likely water and are in no particular hurry to be at any particular point as soon as possible. They have to be sought far and wide in the likely places, and are as uncertain in their reaction to a lure as are any river salmon. The second are the later spring and summer fish which have a definite objective in view in some river at the head or side of the loch and intend to get there without undue delay (I am now, of course, talking of a loch within comparatively easy reach of the sea, and not one in the head waters of a river system). Once their run is finished these fish are much more apt to rise with great freedom to the fly, and to take without hesitation sizes as wide apart as one and one and a half inches. In fact, in one loch where the stock is not large, I think it is possible to get in May at least a rise from every fish as it arrives at its temporary destination at the head of the loch, which, however, is less than ten miles from the sea. Here it is also curious that when the fish will take an inch and a half fly in the loch, they are by no means entirely unsuspicious of one only seven-eighths of an inch long in the short river which connects the loch with the sea. Considerable latitude, therefore, may be exercised in choosing flies for loch fishing, but in later June and July when the wind is not over strong, those of an inch in length will be amply big enough.

Loch water is commonly very clear, and this has to be remembered in choosing a cast. It should err on the thin side, and if it be light for the hook, the gut at the eye should be examined from time to time to see that it is not ' necked.' This clarity of water and the commanding position which one enjoys when standing up in a boat results in one seeing practically every fish as it rises, and sometimes some considerable distance before it reaches the fly. Even if this is not the case the water, not disturbed by any current, usually shows the boil of the fish before it has reached the lure. Consequently, a great deal of self-control is necessary to avoid pulling the fly either out of the fish's mouth or away from it before it has even reached it. It is absolutely necessary that no move to strike be made until the pull of the fish is actually felt on the line : it is better that the rod point be dropped rather than the line tightened when the boil appears, or the fish is seen actually to turn on the fly. Until then, the previous fishing motion should be continued.

Little more remains to be said about loch fishing, except that in playing the fish it should on no account be allowed to get near the boat until practically played out. One so often sees a boat going about a loch with a fish just below the stern where the angler can or does exert little pressure on it, and where, swimming along quietly with its head rather down, it is comparatively comfortable. Directly a fish is hooked, the ordinary boatman pulls in towards it and is terrified lest it run out any of the usually very ample supply of line. His reaction should be the reverse of this. Directly a fish is hooked the boat should be pulled away from it as hard as possible, and a distance of at least twenty-five yards maintained throughout the greater part of the fight.

After all, of what use is one hundred and twenty or more yards of line if none of it is ever used ? If the fish does get rather far away, it will be exhausted all the sooner and, if necessary, the boat can easily be pulled so that line may be recovered. By keeping out a length of line a sideways pull is exerted and the fish is kept on the move, whereas close to the boat it ' stands on its head ' like a sulking fish. In this position the angler has to lift its whole weight, and can do little or nothing with it or to move it. As a matter of fact, if the fish be hooked near the shore and the beach is reasonably clear, much the best fun is to be obtained by going ashore, and the fish will be killed in the quickest possible time. Just at first the boat may be lightly beached and the angler remain on board in case the fish determines to make outwards and refuses to stop, but as soon as it is under reasonable control he may go ashore and select the most promising place at which to bring the fish to the gaff. In doing this he will, if the fates be kind, kill two fish before another angler, who has allowed his fish to come in under the stern of the boat, has had time to kill one.

CHAPTER XIII

MINNOW AND PRAWN FISHING

Minnow fishing usually comes under the generic
term of spinning. Special rods and gear are
required, except for short periods of an occasional
nature when a fly rod may suffice with the necessary
length of line pulled off the reel and held in coils
in the hand, or allowed to trail if the bank be
clear.

A spinning rod need not be as long as a fly rod,
but unless for use in special circumstances should
not be too short. Here, perhaps, it is necessary
to explain that two types of spinning exist. The
one, and older, is used in moderate or heavy water
with comparatively large lures. The other, and
newer, is more suited for water below medium
height, and for correspondingly small lures. A
double-handed rod is normally used for the former
and a single-handed weapon almost invariably for
the latter.

For the heavier spinning, rods from eight feet
six inches to twelve feet may be had, but for the
side cast those nearer the longer length are to be
preferred. For overhead casting shorter rods from
five to six feet long are used. As with a fly rod they
should be suited for the work intended, and probably anyone who intends to spin a great deal in the
spring, when the method receives its greatest reward
and the variations in water-level are extreme, will
want a series of rods built to deal with the heaviest,
medium, and light weights respectively.

The rod which may be of greenheart or split
bamboo as the angler prefers should have a nice
even action throughout. It is a mistake to get

one too heavy for the work it is normally intended
to undertake. A stiff rod is not only 'wooden'
to handle, but is neither so good for casting nor
for playing a fish as a more supple weapon.

For light spinning a rod of from six to eight feet
long may be used, and in this case the remarks as
to a reasonable amount of suppleness apply with
even more force than to the larger rods. An
undue degree of stiffness in this case would, owing
to the light tackle employed, inevitably lead to a
series of lost fish and broken lines or traces.

The friction on the line in spinning is much
greater than in fly fishing, and owing to the necessary
strength of the rod some additional weight on it
is not a drawback. All the rings, therefore, should
be of agate or porcelain, but in either case a pattern
that is well protected by the metal holder should be
chosen. Both porcelain and agate rings are very
easily cracked by a comparatively slight blow, and
they should be examined from time to time to see
that they are still intact.

Of the whole spinning outfit the reel is undoubtedly the most important and, unlike a fly
reel, the most expensive is not necessarily the best.
Spinning reels vary considerably in their essential
principles and therefore in the complication of their
structure, and are priced accordingly.

The oldest and most simple is the free running
Nottingham type which, in the hands of an artiste,
must be a pleasure to use, and is certainly a pleasure
to watch in use. The drum is free running on
the spindle, a check being brought into use after a
fish is hooked, and the most delicate control of
line and length of cast is obtained by breaking on
the run of the flange with the hand. Given free
rein the drum can gather remarkable speed, and
a 'bird's nest' from an overrun can be of corresponding complexity !

The Nottingham reel requires a good deal of
practice and a certain amount of skill in manipu-

lation which is not given to all anglers of limited opportunities. To overcome the disabilities a swivel drum reel was invented which, when turned with what should be the back plate towards the rings, allowed the line to fly off, coil by coil, and all possibility of an overrun was removed. It is again turned to the normal position for reeling in the line. Each coil as it goes off inevitably puts one twist in the line, and these twists are not removed by reversing the drum. Also, for various reasons it will not allow as long a cast as the free running drum type. It has, however, very distinct advantages for many anglers.

In an attempt to avoid some of the difficulties of the free running reels a semi-automatic brake actuated by a lever was invented. The tension of the brake may be varied to accord with the weight used, and the necessary adjustment is easily effected. The use of this reel is much more easily learnt than is that of the Nottingham reel, but the control is perhaps not so fine.

Each type obviously has its advantages and disadvantages, but from the purely fishing point of view there is not a very great deal to choose between them. The individual angler will want to try one of another pattern just to see how they compare with each other.

For all these reels one may have either a dressed silk line of the ordinary fly type but level, or a solid plaited undressed silk line. Personally, I think the latter is to be preferred. It should be dressed before use by immersion in one of the grease preparations sold for the purpose, when the latter is hot. The excess may later be wiped off the line, which will remain in good condition and practically waterproof for a long time. The wear of continual casting causes rather rapid damage to the first few yards which take the initial strain, and this part should be repeatedly tested, and if wanting in strength broken off, during each day.

The reel for the new light bait casting is also of the fixed spool type, but is set permanently in the casting position, and the handle is brought to its proper place (usually on the left, however) through a train of gears. The line flies off free and is returned by means of a revolving setter : at the same time the spool itself moves in and out to ensure an even distribution of the line. In all such reels is incorporated an automatic 'slipping clutch' mechanism with variable tension, so that it is impossible to hold a fish over hard. In some, the line is picked up automatically by the setter after each cast, but in others the angler, by a movement very easily learnt, places it in position with one finger before starting to wind.

Gut substitute instead of silk is sometimes used as a line on the light bait casting reels.

The spools of these reels are wonderfully small, but owing to the thin line employed, are adequate. To reduce friction and facilitate the greatest possible length of cast they should be kept full but not over full. Any appreciable length of line broken off owing to wear should be replaced by a length spliced on, or by a cork 'filler' in the centre of the spool. The outer wall of the spool is only turned over to lessen friction at the top, so that this last point is of particular importance. It is a point which would be worthy of further investigation.

'Killin' wire and piano wire are probably the most popular substances for traces, with gut substitute next and gut the least popular. Wire has the merit of being both stiff (the bait cannot readily fly back and catch up on the trace during the cast) and cheap. A very convenient mounting is to have a swivel and catch of split ring form at one end, a swivel in the middle and a further swivel, to which the line is attached, at the other. The swivel and catch has the disadvantage of allowing the bait to fly back, and perhaps the best, although slightly less convenient mounting, is that used by

Mr. Hutton. In this, one end of the wire is made fast to the eye at the head of the bait and the other to a swivel, to the other side of which is attached twelve or fifteen inches of twisted gut or of gut substitute, between which and the line is inserted another swivel or pair of swivels.

Pliers to deal with the wire should be carried, and the spare wire, on a wooden spool, kept carefully and thoroughly soaked in oil. It is a wise economy to throw away the wire used, keeping, of course, the swivels, at the end of each day. Traces made of Japanese gut substitute throughout may be used until weak on test, but should be dried as carefully as the line.

Of lures three types exist—the devon, a solid metal torpedo-shaped body with a pair of fins at the head : the phantom, of oiled and painted silk, a more or less faithful representation of a fish ; and the natural bait, loach, gudgeon, dace, sprat, sand-eel, etc., usually used with a mechanical mounting to make it also spin. Sometimes, especially in low and clear water, a spoon may be used.

All these lures spin at an apparently high rate of speed, and that is regarded as their chief attraction. They are also to be had in a variety of colours and combinations of colours except the natural baits, though sprats are often dyed a golden tinge. I cannot see that any difference in the various types can exist from the fishes' point of view, and even the fisherman would be hard put to it to decide exactly what lure, or indeed colour of lure, was coming whizzing across the river. Moreover, just two days before writing this I was told by one of our leading ophthalmic surgeons that it is by no means certain that fish have even a rudimentary colour sense. Apart from other practical considerations, therefore, it would appear that the angler may please himself as to the lure he uses. Fresh natural bait may have some attractive smell of which we know not, or formalin may be as repulsive as we suspect, but apart from this it would not appear to matter whether gudgeon or golden sprat, eel tail, or its leather substitute be employed. Spin, with its accompaniment of flash, seem to be undoubtedly the chief attraction.

One variation, however, can be played on this succession of whirring atrocities which too often bristle with triangles, although one at the tail, of a size rather larger than usual, is enough. A natural bait may be used on a non-spinning flight with two sets of triangles, the one on a longer piece of gut than the other, and so arranged that the bait is given a permanent bend or kink. This bait when drawn through the water will wobble rather than spin, and produce a much better illusion of a fish, a somewhat drunken fish it is true, than any other type of lure.

There may be advantages in a lure which slides up the trace when a fish is hooked. Spinning experts argue that this is so, and accordingly prefer the devon type of lure, which is constructed to do this. Some of the other lures and natural bait tackles may also now be found with this conveni-ent feature.

The essence of spinning is that the bait should get right down to the fish which are lying on the bottom. To do this, and for ease of casting, the heavy metal devon, either with or without a lead on the trace, is obviously best. But, sweeping close to the bottom, it is only too apt to be caught up on every snag in the water, unless they be few and their positions known with accuracy. To be sure that the lure is properly down it is better to feel the bottom occasionally, and in somewhat rough places this is more safely done if a phantom or a natural bait be the lure employed, and the greater part of the weight be supplied by a lead or leads on the trace. The lead will then swim slightly deeper than the lure, and allow the latter to clear obstacles which it might otherwise strike.

Phantoms may also be obtained filled with cork, which not only is an aid to casting, but also adds to their floating properties.

Leads may be of a type which is attached directly and evenly along the trace, or which is pendant. The first type is bent into an arc of a circle, and both types refuse to revolve, so that the swivels have to do their work properly and prevent the turns imparted by the fins from running up the line. In Mr. Hutton's mounting the leads are attached to the gut collar between the swivels.

If the bottom be very rough the lead may be attached to a swivel eye with a small piece of gut or thread of convenient strength, so that if it catch up, the fastening will part and only the lead be lost, provided that in the interval the hooks have not also become fast in another snag.

With a short single-handed rod an overhead cast may be used, but the normal cast with the longer spinning rods is a side swing. The trace and a few inches of line are left pendant from the rod point, which is then carried back very slowly round the upstream side of the angler, who at the same time has his weight on the upstream foot and turns until he is nearly three-quarters round from the point to which he is to cast. Rod and body are then returned with gentle but steady acceleration until just as the reel is let go a final flip with the point is given, as if to urge the bait up and over a fence.

Practice will soon show the development of the idea, but a start should be made with a fairly heavy weight. During the earlier attempts spectators should be rigidly excluded from the danger area, for a flying bunch of triangles can do quite a lot of damage, and can land in unexpected places. The angler himself is not even safe, for a jammed reel or a loop thrown round the first ring (a not unlikely contingency with some reels) when only a few yards of line have gone, can result in the lure coming

round in very close proximity to, if not actually
into, the clothing on his back.

The same kinds of water as in fly fishing may be
fished at the different seasons of the year, and the
same precautions may be taken to bring the lure
across slowly or fast, to hang it over the lie, or to
try to tempt the fish to make a dash at it. Time, as
with the fly, should be spent over the better known
and more frequented lies, and the lure should be
not only brought over them a number of times
but also in a variety of fashions. Even more than
in fly fishing each cast should be fished out right to
the end, or until one is absolutely sure that a fish
is not following. They are apt to swim after a
minnow for some considerable distance and fail
to take until they are afraid that the lure is going to
escape them by getting into shallow water or going
out above the surface.

A great variation of speed may be achieved with
a spinning reel, and by varying the amount of lead
used, according to the depth of water and strength
of current. But one of the drawbacks is that the
reel is always in very direct contact with the hooks
and little spring exists to act as a buffer between
the two. Consequently many ' short rises ' and
pulls are experienced, for it is extraordinary how
a salmon can evade even the most complete armoury
of hooks if pull be exerted before it has time to
turn on the lure and properly close its mouth.
Casting across the river so that the lure comes
round with a belly in the line is one way of avoiding
this, but it is, however, not always practicable or
to be recommended. A better method is to always
hold the rod so that it makes as small an angle
with the line as possible. When a straight pull is
inevitable, the rod should invariably be held up,
and if necessary the lure kept down by slackening
the rate of reeling in, so that the full play of the
rod and at least some slight curvature of the line
is available. When a fish is felt it is usually too late

to do anything further about hooking it, for the continuance of the movement of the lure will have done all that is necessary to drive home the hooks which, although comparatively numerous, are not individually large. Striking in these circumstances can do neither good nor harm, though it may hasten the inevitable separation from a lightly hooked fish, and thus save valuable time.

Light minnow fishing, or, as it is sometimes called, thread line fishing, is the counterpart of small fly fishing in low water, and like the latter has enabled the capture of many fish under conditions which formerly would have been considered impossible. In fact, only when the water begins to go out of order in the eyes of the very orthodox does the thread line begin to come into its own.

Light spinning has the advantage of employing not only a light trace but also a line very little thicker or more visible than the trace. Even the finest fly line has to be comparatively substantial and visible for the sake of its casting qualities. A light bait can be cast a long way with a minimum of disturbance, so that even if the lure has to be fished in the path of the line, hope of getting a fish may exist right up until the knot is touching the top ring. Usually the lure should be fished fast, as under those conditions the less the fish see of it the better, and of course it should be of the smallest, no more than trout size.

Objection is sometimes raised that under these conditions a hooked fish plays the angler rather than the angler plays the fish. This, however, should not be, unless the angler be unskilful or the water quite dead and the angler unable to get far enough away from the fish to exert side pressure on it. Even with the lightest tackle the small rod enables a constant strain to be imposed, since the suppleness of the weapon and the general elasticity of the whole outfit, including particularly

9

the slipping clutch of the reel, causes any sudden
strain or jolt to be taken up without accident.

The angler should always keep below or opposite
to the fish so that he is pulling with, and across, the
current.   Unless driven by sheer necessity, he
should never be above it and never allow it to get
so close that his pull is a more or less direct lift.
Then the fish merely puts its head down and to all
appearance is, and remains for a long time, comparatively comfortable.   To keep the fish hustling
about so that it exhausts itself is the ideal, and this
can only be done by the angler also keeping on the
move, so that he is able to exert a pull from a point
downstream of the fish, and with the line at a very
small angle to the surface of the water.   The rod
point held low and the bend taken in a horizontal
instead of a vertical plane is an aid to this last
point.   I would repeat that it is fatal to have the
fish downstream, and especially straight downstream, of the angler's position, and it is equally
bad to let it get into such a position in deep water
that only a lifting pull can be exerted.

A great deal of difference does not exist between
spinning and prawn fishing.   In fact, a prawn
mounted on one or other of the spinning flights
now available is to all intents and purposes merely
a spinning bait.   This form of spinning has perhaps
become more fashionable in recent years, but the
older manner was to mount the prawn on a plain
flight and allow it to travel round after the manner
of a fly, but as slowly and as close to the bottom
as possible.   When the strain of the current is
exercised, some line may sometimes be given instead
of reeled in, so as to keep the bait down to the utmost.
Where it is possible to get right over the lie of the
fish a very slow and rather long sink and draw
motion is very effective.   (I have given elsewhere
in this book an account of the capture of a fish by
this means.)

Another method suitable for rather slow and deep

water is to use a float, either of the primitive after lunch, or elaborate tackle-shop, pattern, in a manner similar to that of the roach fisher. This last practice has for long been popular in parts of Ireland, and was taken up in recent years in at least one English district, where it met with a good deal of criticism and was subsequently barred.

Salmon react rather curiously to a prawn. Sometimes it undoubtedly attracts them as nothing else will. At other times it is not merely negative or repellent, but is actually terrifying. I have never seen the occurrence, but undoubted authorities tell of fish actually leaving a pool into which a prawn is introduced. They are often rather like a dog with a wasp : desperately anxious to bite it, but afraid of being bitten in return. At times in spite of several treble hooks, they seem to be able to take a bite out of the back with surprising delicacy and impunity. In fact, so much is this the case, that it is an open question whether the two or three triangles normally employed might not with advantage be replaced with a single triangle at the stern or with a single hook. Either is certainly a neater and cleaner way of fishing than the multiple hook contrivances. Either is also less likely than the multiple hooks to catch up, which is always a very present danger in prawn fishing owing to the necessity for the slowest possible speed.

Various ways of baiting with a prawn exist. The multiple hook tackles usually consist of a central spear which is passed from the tail upwards into the bait, and the hooks are then stuck on the outside by one of their number, or by a special spear point. A neater mount is obtained with a single hook or single triangle tackle on a link of gut ; the gut is passed through the prawn by means of a baiting needle, and the hook is then drawn up into its proper position. In all cases the prawn is drawn with the ' whiskers ' trailing and with the tail nearest the rod. If desired, the actual tail and one or two segments may be broken off before baiting, but the whole prawn or what remains of it must be securely lashed down with very fine copper wire or red silk. If trouble is experienced in tying the latter, Mr. Chaytor's tip of putting a very small-eyed hook on the free end of the silk and sticking this into the prawn at any convenient point, obviates the difficulty.

The prawn used is of the sizes conventional to the fish market, and may be purchased either fresh or in one of the bottles of pickle sold by the fishing tackle makers. I have, however, preserved the fresh prawns for a long time with a plentiful admixture of salt in a can.

An effective method of summer fishing admirably adapted for the light bait casting rod is with a small prawn commonly known as a pink shrimp. Even in low water salmon do not seem to see too much of a shrimp as they will of a fly or minnow, and therefore the general practice should be to continue to fish it as slowly as possible, especially if the fish are mostly somewhat stale and therefore loth to move far or fast from their lies. Care should be taken that the shrimp is not too big, for if it be, the fish may be definitely scared instead of attracted.

A fly rod is often a more suitable implement for this form of fish : long casting is usually not necessary and with it the shrimp can more easily be held out over the lies of the fish than with the shorter spinning rod.

CHAPTER XIV

WADERS, WADING, AND LANDING FISH

I suppose nothing more primitive exists in these days of progress and civilization than the conventional form of wader. They have the advantage of being easily dried on the inside, but that is their only merit. They are heavy and clumsy, a bother to put on and a nuisance to take off, and when one counts up the cost of brogues, socks, and waders, they are not particularly cheap. The trouble is that for fabric trouser waders no efficient substitute exists : waders, however, and brogues combined are obtainable, very expensive and usually of light construction, and suitable only for the easiest work.

Rubber brogues with leather soles, into which hobnails may be driven and which are both very considerably lighter and also less expensive than the all leather or leather and canvas variety, may now be obtained. These I strongly recommend. But, beware of hooks instead of eyes for the upper part of the lacing ; these, provided in some makes, are a death-trap. Other types require holes to be made in the sides at the instep close to the sole, to let out the contained water when the wearer comes ashore.

The advantage of rubber brogues is that they are both considerably lighter when dry, and when wet carry no absorbed water to add weight when the wearer is on land. Leather brogues, however, may be improved in this respect by plugging the drainage holes with pieces of wood, and soaking them by filling as high as possible with crude castor oil. Repeated occasionally, this treatment keeps them waterproof and always soft, even when

dried after use. The thick sock necessarily worn
between wader and brogue prevents damage to the
rubber from contact with oil. Brogues in the form
of shoes are not to be recommended. They admit
an undue quantity of sand and débris which, in
spite of the thick sock, chafe the wader ; moreover,
they afford no support or protection when wading
among rocks and boulders. For the latter work
many people recommend a thick sole of felt, and
this may be obtained from most tackle shops,
instead of leather and hobnails. It is, I believe,
good though apt to wear rather quickly, but
personally I have never found a plentiful coating of
large nails, renewed before they have worn flat,
fail in the purpose intended, if one wades and
walks with reasonable care.

As to waders themselves (and I now speak of the
' trouser ' variety) it is better to have two pairs,
one of strong, heavy material for use during cold
weather, and the other of much lighter material
for summer wear. The former should be big
enough in foot and leg to allow one to wear an extra
pair of really thick and long stockings reaching up
to the thigh. The long thick stockings worn by
sea fishermen inside their sea boots, and obtainable from their suppliers at the fishing ports, are
very serviceable, comfortable, and warm. For the
lighter waders an extra pair of knitted socks is all
that is required.

Two cardinal faults in a wader are a leg which
is too short and a top which is too narrow. The
inside measurement of the wader leg should be
about five inches longer than the measurement
from the wearer's fork to the ground. When
extended in front, the top of the wader should be
at least six to eight inches from the body. The
braces should be of the same material as the waders,
forming part thereof at the back, and amply long
for crossing at both back and front of body. Inside
the top of the waders, at the front, two pockets

should be made, large enough to carry fly boxes and other odds and ends which one requires while in the water. Two further similar pockets at the back do not come amiss.

Of the short fabric waders nothing need be said. Nothing can be said in their favour when contrasted with the ordinary rubber thigh boot with leather sole, the wader with leather foot and ordinary fabric top, or the waders made of a thin skin of leather inside and an even thinner coating of rubber on the exterior. This last is undoubtedly the lightest and most comfortable wader made : they are but little more tiring to wear than a pair of shoes, but they are undeniably expensive. Some people find difficulty in drying the inside of the foot. This difficulty may be overcome by wearing the so-called non-porous Arctic socks, or the inside of the wader may easily be dried by stuffing the feet after use tightly with newspaper which has been heated before the fire or in the oven. An ample supply of paper must be used and it must be packed in very firmly right to the toe.

Ordinary rubber boots, both of knee and thigh length, have been greatly improved in recent years. The first type with rubber soles was never very good on wet rocks, and rapidly wore smooth and very slippery. Now, however, they may be obtained at a most reasonable price with nails in the soles, or better still, with leather soles and nails. If possible, a pair should be selected with level tops, as the usual top, higher on the outside than on the inside of the leg, is merely a trap for the unwary to allow water an ingress when everything appears to be perfectly safe. These boots have a canvas-like lining (those lined with felt are not recommended) and may be dried like the others mentioned above, but the feet may be thought to be a little hard and provision should therefore be made to allow of the wearing of an extra thick second sock, or, in cold weather, stocking.

A variety of coats for wearing with waders may be seen in the catalogues of tackle- and waterproof-makers. Some button up the front, some are of the over-the-head, ' Poncho ' shape. It is the latter which I prefer, made either of rubber material or oilskin. Oilskin is the lighter and does not absorb water, even on the surface, to add to its weight. The top should fit very snugly about the neck and be absolutely waterproof in front (on a real bad day with wind a very large handkerchief, muffler, or small towel worn inside the collar helps to make a waterproof joint along the top). A second interior cuff with an elastic band to fasten tight should be fitted inside the end of the sleeve for use in wind, and still more in wet, to prevent water running right up one's arm when casting.

For use with long waders, the jacket should come down a few inches below the top of the waders, but only sufficiently far to prevent a gap at this point when one's arms are raised. With short waders the jacket should reach to the knee ; if shorter, it is apt to blow above the top of the wader when walking against a strong wind.

For hats in wet weather, the best are those made of felt with a ' fore and aft ' peak (sometimes called shooting helmets), which resemble a very much overgrown cloth ' deerstalker ' of the old days. For spring fishing a deerstalker with ear-flaps is often a comfort when the northerly breezes blow, and for those with tender hands mittens of one kind or another, or even woollen gloves, are under similar conditions not to be despised.

At other times of the year when the sun shines up or up and across the river, or into one's eyes when loch fishing, a pair of dark glasses is wonderfully helpful.

Almost an essential for wading in rough rivers is a wading staff which may fulfil only its primary purpose, or be a combined staff and gaff. In either event, it should have a large snake ring whipped on to it at a suitable point, by means of which it may be attached to one's person by a dog clip and a loop of cord, or leather strap, placed over one shoulder. The combined instrument is perhaps most useful when fishing unattended. When one is attended by a ghillie the most handy arrangement is a plain staff attached to the person in the manner described, and weighted with lead run when hot into a cavity at the bottom end, so that when free it floats approximately upright.

In either event the bottom should be shod with a rubber crutch ferrule, and not with an iron point which rattles against every stone and rock in the river to warn all and sundry, and presumably the fish also, of one's approach.

I do not know that any particular instructions are necessary about wading. In moderately quiet water with a fairly even bottom, certainly no difficulty should be experienced, however deep one may go—no wading stick is necessary, and only ordinary care in getting a secure hold with one foot before the other is moved is required.

With rapid rivers and a rough bottom it is otherwise. Much more care is then necessary, and unless one is young and surefooted and is, moreover, prepared to take a ducking occasionally, a wading stick is advisable. The Aberdeenshire Dee is probably one of the very worst rivers to wade, for not only is the current swift and the bottom rough, but the stones of all sizes are almost invariably worn through dint of much travelling with the river to a state of glassy smoothness. In a river of this type, there are two golden rules for wading. The first is, always proceed slowly, and the second, always put one's feet on the bottom. The last may seem somewhat unnecessary advice, but what is meant is that one should not be tempted to stand on rocks big or small, off which one may slip or be washed, but should always work one's feet down to the absolute bottom level.

In really fast water it is better always to face the far bank and to progress sideways, never crossing one's legs but keeping the lower leg always downstream, and using the wading stick as an auxiliary support at least while the lower foot is off the bottom. Return upstream should be made in the reverse fashion, working gradually in to, or out from, the bank as is necessary, until one feels the water is shallow enough, or the current sufficiently slack, to allow one to turn. Then, of course, one should always face the current, whether one is going against it or athwart its course.

The current invariably seems to be appreciably stronger when one has to proceed against it than when one is wading with the stream. Further, once the fork of the waders is submerged, the pressure of water and buoyancy of the body, which makes a secure foothold additionally difficult, greatly increase. This must always be kept very prominently in mind when the only convenient point of approach to the shore is upstream.

If one really gets into difficulties the sideways position is of little use. One has then to face downstream, use the wading stick, and in case of dire need the rod also, as a downstream prop and work each foot backwards, inch by inch, until a more comfortable and safer place is attained. It is an unpleasant predicament, and one from which every care should be taken to keep clear. If one is caught by a gravel bank which slides downstream beneath one's feet it is even worse. Then, if one cannot gradually work towards the shore downstream the same procedure has to be adopted, working upstream and, if possible, towards the bank until a more secure foothold is obtained. A great help is not to get excited, but to do everything as slowly and deliberately as possible.

By bad luck or through stepping into a hole one may get into a position from which retreat is impossible, and it becomes necessary to swim for it.

Fortunately, I have never as yet had to do so, but those who have tried say that swimming in waders is not unduly difficult. Whether swimming or floating, one should obviously go with the current, and not try to fight against it, at the same time edging towards shallow water as speedily as possible.

If fishing with a ghillie, landing a fish is a simple business. Once the fish is within reach, he should be encouraged to take the first available opportunity of getting it. No criticism should at the time be offered if he misses the first or any other attempt with the gaff or net, provided it was made reasonably, and with proper skill. The value of the services of a ghillie are much lessened if each fish is completely killed out before he is allowed to land it, and many fish will be lost which might have been killed had they been dealt with when first they came within reach. Even with a ghillie, however, it is a pity to gaff small salmon and grilse if a sloping bank or beach be available, up which they may be hauled, but in this case he should be close at hand, with gaff ready in case the hook comes out at the last minute when the fish is at the edge of the water.

One can often bring a fish a number of times within the reach of a man who is able to move about freely, but when fishing by oneself it is much more difficult to induce it to come near enough to the angler at the business end of the rod. Usually in this event the fish has necessarily to be much more exhausted before it is possible to gaff it, and the use of a net is out of the question.

If permitted by the bank and water, the easiest and quickest method of gaffing when by oneself is to stand quite still in water about knee-deep where the current is slack. The fish then does not seem to realize that the angler is animate and will swim round his knees, where it may very easily be gaffed long before it is exhausted. In fact, so easy is this manœuvre that no special handling of the rod is necessary. But when a fish is gaffed from the bank the rod point should be laid back as far as possible, so that a dragging rather than a lifting force is exerted on the fish. This same theory should be put into practice when a ghillie is employed, and the angler then should not only keep well back from the edge of the water but also finish playing the fish, provided no rocks or other obstructions intervene, with the rod held horizontally (sideways to, and not directly in front of, the angler, of course) rather than vertically.

If shallow water intervene and the angler is without waders, difficulty may be experienced in bringing the fish within reach until it is completely exhausted, and in this case hand lining may materially accelerate the final stages. A clean fish may be hand lined, and may be tailed, as easily and safely as a kelt, provided the precautions mentioned below are observed. Extraordinarily little pressure is also necessary to induce a fish to beach itself when the slope of the bank is relatively flat. Quite a fine cast will suffice to keep the head of even a fairly heavy fish facing inland, so that each flap of its tail takes it farther and farther from the safety of water of sufficient depth for it to swim in.

A kelt should always be landed by means of a landing net, a tailer, or by hand. In the first case it is drawn over the net sunk below the surface and lifted just as in trout fishing. In the second the procedure is very much the same as for gaffing, but the tailer has a noose instead of a gaff hook and this noose is slipped, and drawn tight, over the fish's tail.

Landing the fish by grasping with the hand is commonly known as tailing, and for this the fish has naturally to be played out fully. Usually it is of help if the fish be also hand lined, and indeed this method always materially accelerates matters if it be employed directly the angler is certain that the hooked fish is a kelt.

For hand lining the rod point is held backwards far beyond the ordinary limit until the line leading from the point can be grasped with the left hand. The rod is then laid down with reel handle uppermost and point towards the river, so that the line can run if necessary. If a beach be available, the fish can easily be induced to flap itself up clear of the water, or, if not, it may be held at the side until it is quietly grasped by the hand and lifted on to the bank.

To do this the thumb and first finger should be towards the body of the fish, which must be grasped firmly round the ' wrist ' of the tail by these two and the second finger. The back of the fish is in the V formed by thumb and first finger. The third and fourth fingers must remain loose over the tail, for if the whole hand be closed tightly the tail fin collapses and slides right through the hand. No handkerchief, sand, or other aid is required, and after a very little practice, at first with dead fish ! the operation will be found to be quite easy. The reverse method of holding, with thumb and first finger towards the tail, has been recommended, but, I venture to think, in error. Practical trial of the two will demonstrate which is the better, and a visit to a commercial fish house will show which method is adopted by those accustomed to handle very large numbers of fish each day.

Various methods of gaffing fish have been suggested, and controversy exists as to whether the stroke from above or below is the better. For the beginner, it is undoubtedly easier to place the gaff point (which should be kept quite sharp) uppermost in the water, and to bring the fish over it. This method is sure, but the stroke is made into the soft muscle, which may easily tear if the hold be not adequate or the fish be heavy. The method is also somewhat slow. It is certainly quicker to take the gaff to the fish than the fish to the gaff. The overhead stroke, which should be made not hurriedly but in a decisive fashion and aimed at the shoulder of the fish, is much quicker, and if well executed obtains a much more secure hold. Care should be taken to keep the gaff below the cast, so that the cast is not struck or caught in the bend of the instrument. If the aiming point is too far aft on the fish's body and the fish, as is possible, turns away as the stroke is made, only a few scales will be scraped off and the fight may be prolonged for some time, with possible ultimate loss of the fish itself.

If the fish be foul hooked, particular care must be exercised in inserting the gaff so that a feeble or ill-aimed attempt is not made, and only the fly or bait knocked from its hold. Like everything else, gaffing requires practice, but the basis of a good performance is the stroke made from above with decision but without snatching, into the upper part of the side of the fish.

When on the bank, it is better to grasp the fish by the tail, remove the gaff, and then administer the *coup de grâce*, taking care that should it escape from the hand and the final blow, it cannot readily return to the river. Care should also be taken that the cast is not struck in the course of the proceedings. When, however, it is necessary to kill a fish while the angler is still in the river, *e.g.* after a long wade out to the fishing water, and when further fishing and a rock or other repository for the dead fish is available, it is better to at least stun the fish while it is still on the gaff.

CHAPTER XV

ACCESSORIES AND STORAGE OF GEAR

Of ' gadgets ' there is no end, and the complete
angler may go forth as decorated with them as his
temperament and his purse tempt him to procure.
Some are necessary, some are desirable or helpful,
and some are frankly of no particular use.

A gaff, fly box, minnow and flight box, cast soaker,
and line grease everyone must have. A ' killer '
thermometer, box for flies wet after use, cast case,
a spring balance, and landing net or tailer are
desirable. To enumerate those in the last class would
be unkind to the inventors or makers, but a stone
or file for sharpening blunted hook points and a
record card and fishing book are not among them.

The handiest gaff is a hook on a hazel shaft about
five feet long but, when by oneself, it is a little
awkward to carry, and a collapsible gaff which either
folds in half or telescopes within itself is often taken
in its stead. Only too frequently, however, collapsible gaffs are too short when in use to be efficient
tools. Whether the hook is of the conventional
type or of the Irish type with the central part of
a larger diameter than the rest is of no moment.
For small fish a small gaff hook suffices, and is
indeed perhaps better, but for large fish a large
hook is certainly required, and the shaft should be
adequately strong. A ' tailer,' in which the gaff hook
is replaced by a spring coil of rabbit snare shape,
is sometimes used for kelts or when kelts are about
and is efficient, but a great deal too much is made
of the difficulty of tailing a clean fish or kelt by hand,
and without the aid of gaff or tailer.

The fly book, so beloved of our forefathers, has

completely gone out of fashion, and has been replaced by boxes of copper, tin plate, or aluminium with clips inside to hold each individual fly. The idea is excellent, but in practice the result is not so good. Usually the clips are not sufficiently tempered, do not hold the flies tight enough down, and when subjected to unusual strain after a little wear are apt to become useless. The spacing of the clips, so that each fly sits comfortably without jostling its neighbour, is also a matter of difficulty, and in entering or withdrawing a fly the barb of the hook may be partially or wholly destroyed. At least one firm has tried to overcome this last disadvantage, and to keep the flies in position by making a housing for the point of the hook beside each clip, but this does not do away with the further trouble that the part of the hook under the clip is liable to rust.

The clips should be of a size appropriate to the size of the flies, and it is better that spaces should be left blank rather than that the flies should be overcrowded.

It is as well to mark the top end of each box so that it may be put upright in the pocket, as this helps to keep the flies in their proper positions, and if one possesses several boxes of the same pattern, a coloured line painted with celluloid paint round each helps the angler to pick out quickly the one required.

Various types of minnow and flight boxes may be obtained, but most are rather clumsy to carry at the waterside although admirable for storing the tackle. Certain makes of tobacco are put up in tins which serve excellently for minnows and flights after their primary purpose has been served.

Almost any cast soaking box is as good as another, but if glycerine be added to the water for the felt pads, good rather than harm will be done to the gut.

There is nothing I hate more in fishing than to

see a fish killed by a stone, probably the wrong shape and too small, or the toe of the ghillie's boot. When I do see it, I always hope that the cast, and if possible the hook also, will be broken. The handle of the gaff will do at a pinch (incidentally the wooden handle of a telescopic gaff is very easily broken), but it is very easy to get a piece of heavy wood or to buy one of the very neat small metal or wood and metal killers (or priests), which fit easily into the pocket and which are now available if one has not the facilities for turning a suitable weapon oneself.

The spring balance is always interesting, especially if one endeavours to estimate the weight of the fish before it is put into use. Incidentally a greatly exaggerated idea exists as to the loss of weight after death. This amounts to little more than loss of the surface moisture and normally should not exceed a quarter of a pound at the most in twenty-four hours. Mr. Hutton has shown that the loss in the spring should not normally exceed one per cent in twenty-four hours and perhaps an additional one per cent in the second twenty-four hours.

A thermometer in a revolving brass, or other form of protective case, is an instrument I would be loth to be without. Not only does it give most interesting information as to the river's variation, but it is also of direct practical value in determining the size of fly to be used, not only from day to day, but even at various times during any one day.

Usually one's ghillie, if not stopped, will put the flies when used back into the box still wet—a reprehensible practice. His alternative will be to put them into his own or his master's cap, which is little better. One can now obtain small celluloid boxes, which are excellent for this purpose for all except the very largest flies. These last may find a temporary resting-place in one of those tins of many uses—the small oblong tobacco boxes. From these receptacles each day's selection of flies can

10

be taken and dried at night before return on the following morning to their places in the appropriate boxes.

For carrying one or two small fish a game bag is very handy. If larger numbers are expected, one of those large, soft, basket-like affairs in which carpenters carry their tools is most useful, especially if two leather straps are stitched round it diagonally (with free ends and holes and buckles) to pass over the bearer's shoulders. It is also possible to carry this bag by means of a stick passed through the handles and placed on the shoulder : I have recently seen on the Spey an excellent elaboration of this idea, in which the stick at the bearing point is flat and perhaps three inches broad, with a stuffed leather pad to soften the contact between wood and skin and bone.

A very handy way of carrying a fish is to tie head and tail together with a piece of twine so that the fish is distinctly arched, and then place a piece of stick or other suitable material at the point where the hand grasps the cord. A rabbit snare with twine attached is excellent for the purpose, or a more permanent carrier may be made with a shaped stick and twine with a loop at both ends, the one to form a noose for the tail and the other to pass through the gills from the back, forward to the mouth and over the point of the lower jaw.

In any case the fish, for their own preservation and to prevent contamination of a container, should be wrapped in a damp cloth or other protective material. Incidentally, fish after capture should never be allowed to lie in the sun or wind on the bottom of a boat or on the bank. They should be placed in the shade and covered, so that they are kept damp. It is well to remember, however, that rats and cattle are fond of fish, waterproofs, clothing, and other trifles such as lunch and news-papers, and that washing about in the bilge water of a boat, is not the ideal way of preventing the skin of a fish from drying. After returning home, fish should, if possible, be kept on a stone or concrete floor or slab, previously wetted, and covered with a damp cloth until finally disposed of.

Among minor items are a small, fine file, or the very finest triangular carborundum stone to sharpen dull hook points, and a tin of any of the materials sold by tackle-makers for greasing the line. An angular hook of wood or metal, with twelve to sixteen feet of strong twine attached, may also be carried to release a fly caught up in a tree. One leg of the hook is placed in the top ring of the rod, or very lightly tied to the point. The hook is placed in position on the branch by means of the rod, which is then withdrawn and the branch brought down within reach, if possible, by pulling on the cord. The fly may also sometimes be scraped off by pulling the hook along the branch.

For travelling, rectangular rod boxes made of wood are clumsy, but a great convenience when several rods are carried. For one, a metal or leather protector is serviceable.

One of the charms of angling is to look back on the past. But with increasing years memory is apt to fail without prompting, and the written word recording some past deed will often convince sceptics when oral evidence is not received with the acceptance which we would like to see. A fishing book in which may be recorded one's doings from day to day is therefore indispensable. In it should be stated not only the date and the fish caught but also the pool, name and size of fly or other lure, height and temperature of water in morning and evening, fish risen, pulled, or lost as well as kelts landed, and any general notes which may be thought necessary on the state of weather and so on.

All this sounds rather elaborate and certainly a little determination is sometimes required to put down the facts after a hard day. Gradually, however, a wonderfully complete record of one's sport and its accompaniments is built up, and if one fishes the same water continuously or frequently a mass of valuable detail is accumulated about the most profitable pools, tackle, and methods at all states of the water.

If one is likely to catch many fish in the course of the day, or the details are to be recorded by or for another person in the evening, a score card such as is shown in obverse and reverse in Figures

Name		CAIRNTON.		Date
Pool	Weight	Fly	Size Hook	Time Landed
59144				

Fig. 4.

4 and 5 is very handy for noting the particulars quickly and accurately throughout the day. The original of the card was that used by the late Mr. A. H. E. Wood at Cairnton.

Much gear has to be stored in the winter, or between periods of fishing, in far from ideal conditions. Many of us have neither the room nor the appropriate type of accommodation for everything and we must needs make do therefore with that which is available.

After fishing, all the gear used should first of all be carefully dried. Flies, or minnows, lines, reels, and casts or traces (if not of wire and therefore

thrown away) should all be spread out and left
for at least one night in a dry, warm room where
there is or has been a fire. The rods will have been
wiped down after fishing if necessary. Waders,
waterproofs, and oilskins should be hung in a dry
airy place (on a line in the garden is excellent in
fine weather) and turned as necessary, while brogues

**Measure Hook from bottom of Card,
but do not include loop or eye.**

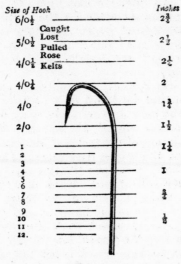

Size of Hook		Inches
6/0½		2¾
	Caught	
5/0½	Lost	2½
	Pulled	
	Rose	
4/0½	Kelts	2¼
4/0¾		2
4/0		1¾
2/0		1½
1		1¼
2		
3		
4		1
5		
6		
7		¾
8		
9		
10		½
11		
12.		

FIG. 5.

should also be put in a similar situation. Gaffs,
and particularly telescopic gaffs, should be dried
and oiled, and if necessary reels likewise should be
taken apart, cleaned, and all bearing surfaces oiled.
This last operation should also be performed once
a week during periods of continuous fishing.

Fly boxes when thoroughly dry should be closed
and stored in any convenient spot. They are
nearly always mothproof, as should be fly storage

cabinets also, so that no special precautions against moths are really necessary although it might be wise to sprinkle a little powdered D.D.T. in them. Special precautions, however, must be taken to protect the feathers used for fly dressing.

Gut if quite dry I find keeps best in an air-tight tin which likewise has been dried by heat ; a particular brand of *crème de menthe* sweets was packed in a round box, air-tight, and of such a size as to be admirably suited for the storage of gut. Failing this cheap and effective container, or some more ornate tin primarily made for the purpose, parchment or greaseproof paper envelopes wrapped in wash-leather or oiled silk so as to make the whole package air-tight are equally good although not quite so handy.

Waders, waterproofs, and oilskins, always fully extended, should be hung in a cool dry place, if possible in the dark and certainly away from strong light which rots almost all fabrics. Waterproof lines must be run off the reel and hung in loose coils also in a cool, shaded, or dark place. The handiest method perhaps is to take the line directly off the reel into small coils in one's hand until the backing is reached, when a loop of the latter is passed through the centre of all the coils and tied to the part of the backing which leads directly from the reel. In this way the dressed line in coils is hung on a loop of the backing which is still fast to the reel. The reels may then be placed on a shelf in a row and the lines suspended by the loops from a row of nails fixed immediately below the reel to which each line belongs. Incidentally, care should always be taken to see that the backing, as well as the dressed line, is thoroughly dried after use, for otherwise, as I once found to my cost, it rots until no stronger than sewing cotton.

Rods should be hung from a nail by the loop on the case, also in a cool, dry place, and all the case lashings should be undone except that at the flap end so that each joint is able to remain free without twist or danger of warping.

The flash of a rod may sometimes be bad for fishing, but nothing looks, or is, worse than an ill-kept rod with broken bindings and worn varnish. Both the latter should be renewed as necessary even if, to please the angler's fancy, the varnish is given a matt finish.

Before attempting to varnish a rod the whippings should be inspected and any which are repaired should receive a coat of spirit varnish. The whole rod, and more particularly so if it has been used with a greased line, should then be thoroughly washed first with warm soap and water and a nail brush (wash well round the rings) and then with plenty of plain warm water ; the ordinary domestic bath, if the powers that be allow, forms an excellent wash tub for the purpose. Afterwards the rod must be very thoroughly dried in a warm room and some good brand of elastic carriage varnish (preferably one specially made for rods) applied in a very thin coat with either a finger tip or very fine camel hair brush. It is then hung in a dry dustproof place to dry and harden ; this will require from two to four weeks. If the varnish does not dry properly in that time the rod probably was not dry, or was dirty or greasy when coated.

Chapter XVI

RIGHTS AND LAW OF FISHING

The principle involved in the right of fishing differs materially in England and Wales and in Scotland respectively. The situation in Ireland also is not exactly akin to that in Great Britain. It will therefore be more convenient to discuss these countries entirely independently.

In England and Wales the right is primarily a *res publica*, and the present status dates back to the time of Magna Charta. Before that revolution was effected the various barons and other landed proprietors no doubt laid claim to all the fishing of any value, but from then on the only private rights, known as ' several fisheries,' recognized are those which were held as being competent and lawful at the time of signing Magna Charta. The result is that almost all the tidal and sea fisheries and possibly some freshwater fishings are public fishings. The Wye, Eden, Derwent (Cumberland), and the Coquet are almost if not quite unique in containing, I understand, none save several fisheries from source to mouth.

The owner of a private fishing necessarily must have access to his water otherwise he could not enjoy the property which he possesses, but unless there be a public right of way or other similar means of access the approach overland to a public salmon fishing may be a matter of some trouble. With tidal but non-estuarial fishings, on the other hand, no such difficulty normally exists.

Private and public rights of both rod and net fishings are fixed entities and not subject to change, but the exercise of these rights in England and

Wales is controlled by the Salmon and Fresh Water Fisheries Act, 1923 (which codified and amended the nineteen previously existing Acts) and various Orders and By-laws made under its provisions.

By this Act each river of importance with adjacent waters constitutes a district under the charge of a Fishery Board, composed of representatives of those interested and of various local authorities, which comes within the purview of the Ministry of Agriculture and Fisheries. The Fishery Boards are financed chiefly from revenue derived from the sale of rod and net licences and in some districts by an assessment levied on the several fisheries also. The officers of the Fishery Boards are responsible for seeing that each angler and netsman has a current and valid licence and that no immature, unclean, or unseasonable fish are retained. Licences may be obtained from the Clerk to each Fishery Board and from a number of distributors through the district. Hotel proprietors in the chief angling centres are normally licence distributors, and in many cases private individuals who are in the habit of having a number of angling guests also keep a stock of licences for the convenience of their visitors.

The salmon rod licence duty in most of the better districts is about £3 for the season with correspondingly smaller sums for a month, week, or day. Every angler must take out a rod licence before starting to fish and a fresh licence is necessary in each new district to which he may go. It is also clearly the duty of every angler to ascertain the limits of the water which he may fish and any arrangement which may have been entered into with the adjoining or opposite proprietors as to the lures that may be used or how any pools, over which a joint right of fishing is exercised, may be fished. On Association waters there may also be laws, written or understood, as to the rotation of fishing and so on.

In England and Wales, although not in Scotland, sea trout rank as brown trout for most purposes and salmon fishing for salmon, trout, or freshwater fish with rod and line may be engaged in on Sunday, but the annual close season may vary from district to district and being established in each case by by-law may be altered, within certain limits, by revision of the by-law. The addresses of the Clerks to the Fishery Boards and the dates of the open seasons used to be published in the annual report on the freshwater fisheries of the Ministry of Agriculture and Fisheries, but this practice was discontinued in recent years. In any case of doubt the information, however, could be obtained from the Ministry by correspondence.

Immature salmon, that is parr and smolts, and unclean and unseasonable salmon if caught may not be retained but must be returned to the water alive and as far as is possible uninjured. Kelts also should not be gaffed, and parr and smolts should be unhooked carefully. Normally no great harm is done to the fish by the experience of being played and landed, but if unfortunately a smolt or kelt is hooked in the gills so that the gills bleed when the hook is removed nothing will save the life of that fish. Even if returned to the water at once it will speedily bleed to death.

Unclean and unseasonable salmon are those which are about to spawn, are spawning, or have spawned and have not yet returned to the sea. The definition of the first class is exceedingly difficult, and although various attempts have been made to set up a form of words which will meet the situation it is practically impossible to draw a hard and fast line of division. It may be presumed, however, that ripe but unspawned fish—generally known as baggots or rawners—captured after the opening of the new season in the spring may be classed as definitely unclean. Spawning fish, owing to the circumstances in which they are taken, present no difficulty, nor in general do spawned fish which are usually known as kelts.

Kelts are not often difficult to detect, especially early in the season. They then still carry much of their spawning livery (unless they have entered the river very late indeed) and this alone, apart from their thinness, distinguishes them from clean salmon. By March, however, most of the kelts are distinctly silvery. Later they are as bright as the incoming fish and much brighter than clean winter salmon which have been in fresh water for some months. This renewed brightness, rather hard and metallic when compared with that of a clean fish, is accompanied by an apparent improvement in the condition, but this appearance of fatness is entirely illusory and weight actually continues to be lost until the fish returns to salt water. In all about one-third of the total weight is lost between the fresh run and the kelt stages.

Sometimes an exceptionally good kelt or an unusually thin clean fish may raise doubts in the mind of the captor, and then a careful inspection must be made as rapidly as possible. If the fish can be laid on a dark flat surface such as the bottom or seat of a boat or fishing hut, or on a plank on the shore, judgment will be facilitated. In the middle section of a kelt the dorsal and ventral contours are nearly parallel, whereas in a clean fish, however thin, they are both distinctly convex. A kelt's fins and tail are always thin near the ' root ' where they join the body and are often somewhat worn and frayed ; the scaled surface of the body also has a somewhat different appearance to that of the sleek springer. The crustacean parasites, *Lernaeopoda salmonea*, in the gills which masquerade under the name of gill maggots, are no guide, for although practically every kelt has some, or more usually many, of them, clean winter salmon soon acquire them. The small proportion of clean fish which are on their second or subsequent return to spawn also still carry the survivors of their first sojourn in the river.

Snatching and stroke hauling—that is, fishing with a legal lure or bare hook so that the hook is driven into a fish which is passive in the water is, of course, illegal as well as unsportsmanlike, just as is gaffing or netting a fish which has not been hooked and is not sick or dead.

In Scotland the right of salmon fishing in river, estuary, or sea is the private property either of the Crown or of an individual. Sea trout in this country for the purposes of both the right of fishing and the law regarding the exercise of the privilege are counted as salmon. Contrary to the belief held by some, therefore, free or public fishing does not exist and even sea trout fishing in sea or estuary is incompetent and illegal without the permission of the owner. Incidentally, however, a public right of fishing for brown trout exists in tidal and navigable waters, but in such situations not many brown trout are likely to be found.

Where the Crown is the owner of salmon fishings in Scotland it holds the right not *pro bono publico* but for value and it is from the Crown that title to all salmon fishing in the country flows. Salmon fishing formed originally part of the private revenue of the Scottish kings, and where the title is now in private possession it was originally granted for services rendered or value received. Now, however, the Crown no longer sells what remains of its holdings, whether net or rod fishing be involved, but lets them to the highest bidder and the rents go into the general revenue of the country.

The law which regulates salmon fishing in Scotland is much older than that of England and of both Northern and Southern Ireland. It should, however, be brought up to date as soon as possible. The chief existing statutes were enacted in 1844, 1862, and 1868, and in general broad principles so far as the angler is concerned do not differ markedly from the English position.

Each river is, in theory, under a District Board composed entirely of proprietors, and each Board is responsible for the administration of the law in its own district just as are the equivalent bodies in England. The central authority in Scotland corresponding to the Ministry of Agriculture and Fisheries in England is the Fisheries Division of the Scottish Home Department, whose office is in Edinburgh.

The chief points of difference in practice between the two countries are that in Scotland Sunday fishing for salmon and sea trout, although not for brown trout, is illegal and rod licences are not at present required. The District Boards obtain all their revenue from direct assessment on the fishery owners alone.

Each district in Scotland has its own close time which is regulated by by-law, and lists of these dates together with the names and addresses of the District Board Clerks will be found in the annual reports of the Fisheries Division. The Border Esk, although to a large extent running through Scotland, is for legal and administrative purposes regarded as being entirely in England and it is subject to the English 1923 Act. That other Border river, the Tweed, is dealt with by its own statutes made in 1857 and 1859, which provide certain differences from both England and Scotland in the local supervisory body and permit of the killing of sea trout kelts and baggots at all times and of smolts also in every month except April and May. These last-mentioned exceptions to the general rule, are, of course, difficult to defend in the general interest.

In both Northern Ireland and the Irish Free State the ownership of rod fishings is exactly the same as in Scotland except that public fisheries may exist in certain of the Free State estuaries. In both

countries rod licences are necessary, but if issued in
one district may be extended for use in others by
the payment of an additional sum which is less than
the full figure. In both countries as in Scotland
and England the intentional killing of kelt is illegal,
but in the Free State, Sunday fishing is permitted
although not in Northern Ireland.

When an owner has only one side of a river the
usual boundary is the *medium filum* or middle of the
stream. This line is not always ascertained with
ease and certainty. Islands, banks dry when the
river is low, numerous channels and so on com-
plicate the position, but each such case can only
be decided on its merits and sometimes only after
reference to a court of law—an expensive and,
when between neighbours, not always an advisable
course. In narrow rivers such division must
obviously make angling somewhat difficult. It is
then desirable to arrange to fish so that an angler
on each side is not on the water at the same time
or that each proprietor should have undivided and
uninterrupted possession for three days of each week
with, if Sunday fishing be permissible, alternate
Sundays.

The upper boundary of a fishing obviously forms
the upper limit for the angler for, although he must
be allowed to have sufficient access for the reasonable
enjoyment of the property, this could hardly be held
to extend (apart from access to the waterside)
to property not opposite the fishing. Casting
square across would seem to afford ' reasonable
enjoyment ' of the few uppermost yards of the
water. Some authorities, in Scotland at least, have
held that as regards the lower boundary an angler
standing on the limit may continue to fish as far
as he can cast downstream, but, whatever the
courts might have to say to this dictum, the practice,
especially with modern bait casting outfits, can
scarcely be commended on the grounds of sports-
manship or as likely to encourage a happy and

desirable state of good feeling between the proprietors concerned.

In the case of loch fishing, unless the loch be of
special shape and the boundaries of convenient
relationship thereto, it is almost impossible to divide
the water into separate parcels each confined to
one individual proprietor. A right of fishing on a
loch, therefore, is usually held to extend to the whole
loch and the fishing over the whole of the water is
considered to be one property which all the proprietors concerned share jointly unless there be
express reservation to the contrary. For instance,
in some cases one proprietor owns a loch but
another, and perhaps more than one, has the
right of one, or more than one, boats' fishing
thereon.

In England the right of salmon fishing normally
goes with the adjoining land provided the owner
of the land has also sufficient title to the fishing,
but, of course, title to the fishing can be separately
conveyed. But in Ireland and Scotland this is not
necessarily the case. In Scotland the right of salmon
fishing is a separate heritable property subject to
a title quite apart from that of the land which it
may adjoin. In many cases the owner of the land
has no right at all to cast line on the water for
salmon. This right may belong to the Crown or
to some other individual, although the right of
brown trout fishing is inseparable from the land.

In all cases the right is solely the right to the
fishing ; there is no right to the fish until they are
captured ;

Chapter XVII

RIVER IMPROVEMENTS

Nature has provided us with rivers and fish to stock them. Sometimes she has been generous and given the best possible conditions for the reproduction and maintenance of a large stock. At other times from one cause or another she has restricted the salmon population to much smaller proportions than we expect and below that which, in our more exalted moments, we think might be obtained. Often man has stepped in and by interfering with Nature's arrangements has curtailed the supply of salmon far below that which was intended for his support and enjoyment not merely as a sport but as a food supply and an industry.

If one dealt with the subject of river improvements in its widest sense one might easily fill a volume and then not have treated it too profusely. Within its ambit might be included such very wide fields as pollution, the regulation of netting in accordance with the capacity of the district, facilitating the passage of fish over obstructions both natural and artificial, and the controversial and open question of the gain to be obtained by the improvement of natural hatching facilities in the river or by the provision of a hatchery.

This present treatise is hardly the place to discuss any of these questions even if space permitted. Pollutions provide a highly technical subject and moreover one of high policy also. The regulation of netting in detail, apart from questions of broad policy, can only be settled after careful inquiry in each district. There are, it is true, certain general principles which can be laid down for the con-

J. E. Young.

A NEW SALMON PASS. TONGLAND DAM.
RIVER DEE (SOLWAY).

W. J. M. Menzies.

AN OLD SALMON PASS. DEANSTON DAM.
RIVER TEITH. CONSTRUCTED 1828.

struction of fish passes, the chief being that the mouth (*i.e.* the bottom) of the pass should be absolutely in the right position, but that again is a technical subject more suited for a technical publication. The construction of a pass also is not usually a matter for an individual proprietor, unless he be the owner of the obstruction, but for the board of the district or a combination of proprietors.

In the absence of definite experiment and proof one can only advance the arguments for and against the establishment of a hatchery to deal with ova of salmon from the river on which the hatchery is situated. First of all it is necessary to point out that all the ova in such a hatchery, as is too commonly assumed, is not a gain to the river. The gain, if any, is only the amount by which the artificial processes are more successful than Nature would be if left to her own ways.

There are in fact two very clearly marked divisions in hatchery work. In the one, ova is imported into a river from another district. In the other, only ova taken from fish in the district in question is treated.

With regard to the first transaction there can be no question. The district undoubtedly benefits but it is by no means certain to what extent. It is probable that something of the order of one adult fish per thousand ova brought in is about the gain which accrues to the river.

It is the second transaction which is open to dispute, and the gain to be derived from the small hatcheries holding one million ova or less which are at present in use is certainly problematical. The size alone of such a hatchery, on a river with even a comparatively reasonable stock of fish, is small. We can perhaps realize this a little better if we try to visualize the total number of fish which spawn and then recollect that each female sheds about six to seven hundred eggs for every pound of her weight. Even if the return of adult fish were

doubled from that particular set of eggs the benefit
would not be very great, and this result is problematical with the present methods of distribution
of fry and often the lack of correlation between the
temperature of the water in the hatchery and of
that in the tributaries where the fry ought to be
placed. The stage at which feeding is commenced
is undoubtedly one of the most critical in the whole
life of the fish and one at which really colossal
losses may occur. Luck or lack of luck at this
particular point may make or mar the success of
a whole season's hatching, and it is undoubtedly a
point which requires the most careful consideration
when establishing a hatchery.

Only a complete experiment which has been
suggested and to some extent planned but which
as yet has not been put into operation can prove
the position which artificial hatching ought to
occupy in our salmon fishery organization. It is
an experiment with a very direct economic bearing
on both the commercial and sporting fishings, and
until it is carried out it is impossible to offer advice
of a definite and general kind on the question.

So far as we can see at present on the ordinary
river where the natural spawning grounds are
abundant and practically the whole of the tributaries
are available to the fish we have not sufficient data
to recommend expenditure on a hatchery. On the
other hand, in a district where much fry and parr
feeding ground is inaccessible to the fish owing
to obstructions, or the natural spawning ground is
deficient (or liable to damage) when compared
with the fry and parr feeding capacity, as in some
of our smaller Scottish districts, then in all probability the establishment of a hatchery might be
of some considerable benefit. In the one case the
fry could be placed in what to salmon is virgin
feeding ground, and in the other much ova would
probably be saved from destruction by winter
spates and other causes and the fry could be spread

out over a considerably greater area than would be the case were they to be confined within the radius of the available and safe natural spawning grounds.

The subject which perhaps might most appropriately be discussed for a short space in this volume is the actual improvement of fishing waters either by the construction of works to induce the fish to lie and to take more readily, or to provide additional water to induce the fish to run or to rise. A further consideration is the maintenance of banks and works to prevent the deterioration of existing conditions.

Before commencing any improvements if one possesses fishing on only one side of the river it is advisable and indeed necessary to obtain the concurrence of the proprietor of the water on the side opposite to the proposed alterations whether they be of a minor or of a major character. A little preliminary discussion and adjustment and some give and take may save a lot of future friction and trouble, and in the end be of mutual benefit. Also any works must not actively interfere with the passage of fish to the waters upstream.

The most simple form of improvement is to provide lies behind or alongside which fish may rest. Even in slack water they do not like a smooth bottom but prefer some object near which they may remain. It is as if they felt the need for cover, and indeed in low water and shallow pools they will show this feeling by seeking holes in among the rocks and under the bank into which they may retreat like a lobster or a fox. To complete a very mixed natural history bag they, however, also follow the reputed habits of the ostrich, for once their head is hidden they are quite unconcerned about their tails which, if the hole be not long enough to accommodate the whole of their body, they leave protruding in a most visible manner. This is the poacher's opportunity for they then may be ' guddled ' like trout, and even do not object to being drawn out of their hiding-place backwards, although once put off an even keel their opposition immediately becomes pronounced. Lest unwarranted inferences be drawn from this apparently intimate acquaintance with the subject, I hasten to add that I learnt the details of this particular performance when catching fish for the purpose of marking them !

The best form of imported ' lie ' is undoubtedly a natural rock well worn and moss grown and not newly dug up and light coloured. Fish are not happy with white or light-coloured objects in the water, and considerably greater time is required to mature a light-coloured stone in the river than might be thought necessary.

Failing natural stone a concrete block serves the purpose well, but for the reason just mentioned the concrete should be coloured with one of the preparations which are now sold for the purpose.

Undoubtedly the ideal shape for a stone or concrete block is approximately that of an egg with the thicker end upstream. Fish can then easily please themselves as to whether they will lie behind the obstruction or alongside with their noses just projecting beyond the bulge. They may even prefer to be upstream with their tails almost resting on the upper edge of the stone. Those in the two latter positions are more likely to take a lure than are those actually downstream of the lie. Concrete should be cast without any angular edges and one or two eyebolts set in while it is soft may materially facilitate handling later.

A stone or block of quite modest dimensions is of astonishing weight, and the only advice one can give as to size is that those used should be as large as will fit the pool or river and can be handled. Care should be used in setting the lie so as to get it into correct alignment with the stream. The long axis should be exactly parallel with the current and not by any means athwart it. If it be not exactly parallel with the run of the water the confused current which results may well not be to the liking of the fish and may also interfere with the proper working of the fly when passing over it.

If the water be too deep to wade (a bathing suit instead of waders may in any case be useful) this desirable precision may be difficult to obtain. In such circumstance it is probably easiest to run the stone or block up on to the stern of a coble or on to planks set between two boats and then put it over the side when the boat has been moored and fixed exactly in position. If two eyebolts be cast in the concrete block, one towards each end, or similarly set in a stone, and ropes are rove through them before the lie is let go into the water, then its position can afterwards be trimmed by hauling on the ropes, which may ultimately be recovered by allowing one end to go free and pulling on the other.

A so-called water telescope is of great assistance when setting lies or for general inspection of the river bed. The essential idea of this instrument is merely to get rid of the surface refraction and ripple, and its use makes a quite astonishing difference to the clearness of the view. Its construction is quite simple. A rectangular tube of wood or a circular tube of metal about two feet long, open at both ends and of a diameter just sufficient to admit one's face comfortably is all that is required. The bottom may be closed with a sheet of glass but it is of no particular advantage and if it becomes misty on the inside it is an actual disadvantage. The bottom is immersed below the surface and one looks through the top end excluding by one's head or other means all extraneous light so far as may be possible.

In shallow water a lie may be worked into exact position with crowbars or long levers of wood. When the river is dead low it may sometimes be worked right from the bank to its final position in this manner. Another method is to get a grip with a pair of stonemason's shears and then haul from the far side of the water or other convenient position with a long rope passed through the handles of the shears.

Although I have referred only to stones and concrete blocks, an even better material in some cases is formed by a gravel and wire-netting pillow such as is described a little later in this chapter for croy and dam building. If in water which at times is shallow such pillows can be constructed *in situ*, or they can very easily be built up on a boat or raft which is afloat in the water and then the pillow sunk in position when it is completed. Their shape and size is more easily controlled than is that of a stone or concrete and their construction is quite simple. Their only drawback is that a fly or minnow might very occasionally be lost by being caught in the wire but where they are used I have yet to hear of such a happening.

Little can be said about the actual selection of the position for a lie. So much depends upon the minute details of the local geography of the water that generalization is of little help. It is to be presumed, however, that anyone who indulges in this work will have had some experience of angling and of the apparent likes and dislikes of the fish. Advice from the more skilled can also usually be obtained, and some amusement may be derived by calling together an informal committee of one's friends for consultation before the work proceeds.

In water of moderate depth without many lies salmon usually seek the deepest part, but may usefully be induced to stay on the shelving and not too shallow sides by placing lies there. Just on the edge of strong streams is another favourite place and after a longish run up a shallow reach they are also fond of seeking a lie in the tail of the next pool with all convenient speed.

If the pool or stream be rather smooth bottomed and featureless, lies may be scattered anywhere about the deeper part, choosing if possible hard, well-consolidated ground rather than gravel which is liable to move. But in this work one must always bear in mind the type of fish one wishes to invite to stay. It is obviously no good putting lies for spring fish in a strong stream or for grilse in a slack dead part of a pool when there is a stream or more lively water available. One must always bear in mind the fish's natural choice and act in accordance therewith.

In writing generally I have necessarily only been able to mention a few of the possible places where reward might be rapid. Sometimes several stones may be placed in line ahead, that is more or less directly ahead of one another, with, say, an interval of not less than ten feet between each. Or they may be similarly placed but in echelon. At other times a nest of three or four will yield better results than any other grouping. And so on, but a little thinking and ingenuity and some trial and error will in the course of two or three seasons show how best the fish may be made to respond to one's efforts.

Another use to which stones or blocks may be put is directing the course of a stream. They may be used to spread or to concentrate the water or to direct it, so far as may be possible, towards any desired point. For this purpose stones, concrete blocks, or gravel pillows have to be fairly large and their exact shape is not of great moment. They are suitable also for use only in the smaller type of waters. In the larger streams a single stone would not have enough effect, and control must then be exercised by a croy or similar structure.

In strong water the permanence of the position of a lie is assisted if a hole be excavated into which its lower part will fit. Unless the ground reached be very soft and liable to further excavation by the water it is scarcely necessary to make up the hole round the sides of the lie since the first flood will usually bring down enough débris to do this work.

The excavation of a hole may also be a promising method of forming a lie for a fish especially at the tail or side of a run. This must, however, be done with discretion as, once started, the continuations may be almost out of control. Most pools and situations suitable for this operation have a rather smooth bottom not of rock. Commonly such bottoms consist of a fairly hard crust with a some-what soft sub-stratum. Once the crust is broken the water may continue to work and extend the hole very considerably. This may be a not alto-gether bad thing at the site but the débris may be carried down and, deposited in a quite undesired place, may fill up existing lies or do a pool farther down the river no good. On the other hand, the hole may fill up ; then only the labour expended on making it is lost. The excavation may be started with a crow-bar or similar implement to break the surface. A ' muck rake,' that rake-like tool with three or four strong prongs bent at right angles to the line of the shaft, is also most useful, as is naturally a fork, spade, and shovel. Gravel may also be dragged out by means of a tool like a mussel or oyster dredge with a rectangular iron frame (if possible the bottom should be of flat iron made to dig in) and a wire-netting bag to hold the stones which are scraped up as the imple-ment is dragged on its bottom edge along the bottom.

For the larger river improvement operations, such as the construction of croys or dams and the pro-tection of banks, people are too apt to think in terms of concrete. This in itself is an excellent substance and one sees some really remarkable structures to hold water constructed of it. But it requires to be made and set with some care and skill and to be placed on a quite solid permanent foundation. Without this last, often somewhat expensive, preparation concrete is apt to crack, then to break up into sections, and finally to travel down the river on the first really big flood. All over Scotland I see traces of this development in some fragments of concrete still clinging to the bank at the original site of the structure or others cast about the river.

What is required for such work unless it can be sited on good rock and put in ' in the dry,' as the engineers have it, is something flexible that will, within limits, conform to local movements and which when some slight erosion does take place will sink in and help to stop further attrition instead of being left suspended in the air and assisting, by concentration of the water, in widening the breach. Structures, moreover, that look admirable when the river is low become puny and inefficient in the extreme when the water rises and a flood bears down on them.

The old-fashioned method of building a dam is similar to the walls so familiar and known as ' dry stone dykes,' in Scotland. One sees these everywhere in mill dams, fishing cruives, and croys too. They require careful building not only as to the form which will best resist the flow of the water but also so that the stones are properly fitted in and interlock the one with the other. No cement is used in their construction, and at first the whole structure is more or less porous but soon it gets filled up on the upstream side with sand, gravel, and other débris. When properly made on a good solid foundation a croy well built after this fashion is excellent, and if the slight repairs necessary each spring are duly attended to it will last for very many years indeed. On a gravel bottom, however, such a structure is apt to break up and be washed apart owing to the inevitable movement of the foundation.

On a gravel or moving bottom and indeed in

any place where large stones and rocks are not available, a wire-netting ' pillow ' or ' bolster ' of the appropriate shape and size is undoubtedly the best.   This form of protection for railway embankments is used in Switzerland and elsewhere on the Continent, but for the introduction of the idea for our rivers I believe we are indebted to Colonel A. D. G. Gardyne, of Aros, Mull.   Both the principle and the actual work are simple.   A sheet of square mesh wire netting of the appropriate size (4 or 5 inch mesh and 5 or 6 gauge wire are most suitable) is laid in the desired position, sufficient stones or gravel are placed on it by barrow, cart, or other means and the netting is then brought over the heap and laced up with soft but stout seizing wire.   The final result is a wire-netting bag of stones which is both heavy and flexible so that it conforms, and continues to conform, precisely to the shape of its bed and is of exactly the right size and figure. For a croy or a dam, two, three, or more bolsters may be used so as to overlap and interlock to form a solid whole with such base and taper as may be necessary.   An additional bolster may be placed as an apron to prevent undue erosion on the downstream side if required.

In some places where the river bed is peat or soft soil a croy is perhaps most usefully and easily constructed by driving in two rows of piles (larch fencing posts of the right size and length serve the purpose) from two to three feet apart, placing boards on the inside of each row and at the end, and then filling the interspace with stones, stones and peat well trampled down, or any other suitable and available material.

A croy, which is in effect a dam built out from the bank, may be of any length, height, and size and may serve three purposes.   It may divert or concentrate the waterflow, provide a stance for the fisherman or lies for the fish.   But whatever the purpose the construction is essentially the same.

The chief difference which exists between well-constructed croys, apart from the materials of which they may be made, is the angle at which they are set to the river. Many will be found to be sloping at an angle downstream—that is, at an acute angle with the bank from which they project. Some are at right angles to the bank. A few may sometimes be seen to be set very slightly in an upstream direction.

At first sight the downstream angle seems to be both natural and likely to be best. But if we examine the results we see that although it leads off the water with a minimum strain on the structure yet a very considerable eddy may be set up below the point of the croy and between it and the bank. This eddy not only excavates a very large hole if the bottom be at all soft but at the same time may cut seriously into the bank itself. The eddy is, of course, usually of no use for fishing, although often fish will lie just along the line where it joins the main stream coming off the croy.

On the other hand, croys set both at right angles and upstream (though the angle in the latter case must be very small indeed) do not lead to the formation of serious eddies or the excavation of bed or bank. In their case the water either passes the end with the minimum of eddy formation or at higher levels (when the damage at the downstream inclined structures is chiefly done) ; when the water is going over the top it chiefly passes straight on downstream without being materially diverted from its course.

Croys made to divert or control the direction of a stream may very often not be joined actually to a bank. In such situations there is often a considerable stretch of gravel or other material between water and land at the normal flows, and obvious advantages exist in not making a complete structure. In no case should a croy be made higher than is necessary at the water-levels when it will be of use.

If too long or too high, unexpected and unpleasant results may occur during flood flows.

A great many experiments of a most instructive and interesting kind may be made in the construction of croys intended to encourage fish to rest. I can recall an admirable example of an almost perfect effect produced in the moderately deep water of the middle section of a long and rather evenly flowing pool. The croy at right angles to the bank cut off the stream for the whole length of the structure and projected it as a line of moving water just alongside the practically still area. The bottom was moderately rough and the junction of stream and still provided just the conditions in which spring fish love to lie. Incidentally this croy terminated at its outer end in that best of all anchors, a very large natural rock which obviously must have been in its present position for a very long time.

Another rather similar croy on the same water in a pool where the current is directed slightly in towards the bank had not produced quite such a complete result but had provided an excellent taking place just where the current again began to have a free run in towards the bank.

One can often cause a considerable deepening of the water off the point of, and below, a croy when the bottom is of loose material. Fish delight to lie in such situations though not willing to do so when the water is cold unless the excavation be sufficient to allow them to get into completely slack water free of the current right at the bottom. Incidentally when this is likely to occur steps should be taken to see that the end of the croy does not gradually fall into the newly made hole. If a large boulder, long in its site, can be chosen so that the croy may be built out to it then whatever happens the position is reasonably secure.

Grilse and summer fish usually like to lie off the point of a croy or in the stream below rather than in the junction of the waters. For their benefit, therefore, lies, which need not be large or they will perhaps spoil the run of the stream, may be placed in suitable positions down the line of the current.

Croys of quite simple type, *e.g.* posts and logs or even hurdles, may be used to move or arrange banks of mud and other soft material, but these are more suitable for the quieter south country spring-fed trout streams than the more turbulent salmon rivers.

When croys are intended as convenient stances for anglers the top may be made on a slope from the land end downwards so that as the water rises some at least may still be available. In fact, all croys may be of this form although no great advantage is derived from it ; indeed, disadvantage may accrue if the additional obstruction and concentration of water puts the lies out of commission too soon when the river rises.

Rather than make a croy too high it is better to construct stepping-stones along it or a bridge on rough piling from which fishing may be conducted. Cross pieces of wood, or some other anti-slip device, however, should be nailed to the surface of the wood. If the water and position be at all dangerous a handrail should also be provided, not too high so as to interfere with casting, but on the other hand not as low as one I have seen. It was little more than knee-high and seemed to make a toss into the river absolutely certain if one slipped or leant over too far.

A further device to assist casting is to have a single plank bridge extending out to a rock on which the angler may stand ; it is surprising what an assistance an extra distance of only two or three yards from trees or a high bank may be or how much it may facilitate reaching a lie rather far off. If there be danger of the plank being in the way when a fish is being played or of it carrying away in a flood it may be arranged to slide in and out as required or to pull over (by means of a cord or chain) on a

hinge at the land end. In the latter event bronze
and rustless steel are obviously indicated for the
metal parts. In passing it may be said that very
often advantage is not taken of this plank-to-rock
bridge which is so easy and inexpensive to construct.

The protection of river banks is a subject not
directly connected with fishing, but one very often
of paramount importance to the fishery owner.
The favourite construction for this work is pile
and plank or pile and wattle, and too often the owner
spoils not the ship for a ha'porth of tar but the
whole of perhaps heavy expenditure for the sake of
a few more pounds. Every angler must be able
to recall place after place where a line of such
piling can be seen still in relatively good order,
but with water behind as well as in front of it and
not at all fulfilling its original purpose. Piling
is good in its way and if properly completed fairly
efficient, but a mere line of work along the threatened
part of the bank does not constitute proper completion. At both the up- and downstream ends the
piling should be turned inwards and continued, in
a trench if necessary, until there is no danger of the
biggest flood getting round the ends and cutting
in from the upstream side or eating in from the
downstream end. The bank above the top of the
piling should also be protected up to above
flood-level by piles, rails, and fascines (brushwood),
loose big stones or other material which the water
cannot damage. If on a fairly easy slope turf
may do, but it should be held down with wire netting
fastened to posts driven flush into the ground.
Cattle and sheep should be rigorously kept off all
bank protection works, which should also be regu-
larly inspected. Here if anywhere a stitch in time
saves nine, and the small erosion of one flood may
easily become the yawning gap of the next if not
sealed and protected at once.

When piling is not necessary or for any reason
not advisable, large (but they must be really large)

stones may be cast in loose so that they conform exactly to the bank and settle in without any further movement. Such protection, however, like piling, must be adequate and complete at both the up- and downstream ends and up the bank as well. An even more effective, if much more expensive, method is to pave the bank with smooth-faced stones, but cost alone probably puts this out of court in these days.

The pegged-down wire netting mentioned in connection with piling, may alone sometimes be a help. It may also be of decided assistance in controlling a gravel bank which is given to movement and which for any reason it is desired to stabilize. If it be possible to start the growth of grass on such a bank the chances of stability and permanence will be much increased.

Dams at the exit of existing, or to create new, lakes for water storage purposes may, if of reasonable size, be made of gravel and wire-netting pillows, dry-stone dyke construction, or of concrete. For larger structures the latter material is necessary, but in certain situations at all events the provisions of the Act concerning the safety of reservoir works may be operative and inquiries regarding this should be made.

There can be no doubt that the possibility of releasing floods to attract fish from the sea or of sufficient water to keep the river at a good fishing level beyond the natural time adds very materially to the chances of sport and to the value of the fishing. Either proceeding must, however, be followed with some care and thought.

It is obviously of no use, for instance, to release a flood when no fish are at the mouth of the river or when those that were there have temporarily left owing to a change of wind or other cause. A flood to attract fish should reach the sea at the time of tidal high water and when the wind is blowing on to the shore as well as when it is believed that fish are in the near neighbourhood of the river mouth.

If a natural flood has run its course for some time it is probably of no great advantage immediately to keep the river running at the best fishing height. Salmon after a time become stale and listless if the water remains at one level even if that level may normally provide the best sport. It is better therefore that the level should periodically be varied. For a short time it might be allowed to fall low and then the fish re-awakened to activity by raising it to the best height or, to induce them to move from pool to pool, a modest flood might be released and from that the water allowed to fall away gradually. Again, with an ample natural supply which had been running for some time the effect of control could be tried by shutting the sluices and storing as much as is possible until the reservoir is quite full.

Unless no possibility of damage from a breakaway exists, the construction of a dam at a lake should only be undertaken after full consideration and in any case of doubt after consultation with a competent engineer. It is generally a case in which the co-operation of a fishery adviser and an engineer is highly desirable.

P. R. C. Macfarlane.

A MALE KELT.

John Douglas.

A FRESH SALMON AT SELKIRK CAULD.

CHAPTER XVIII

THE LIFE OF THE SALMON

One is commonly greeted with the remark that
we know little or nothing about the life of the
salmon. With this statement I profoundly disagree.
We may know little about the reason why a salmon
takes a lure and not much more about its destination
during its sea life. But for the rest we really know
what is almost a remarkable amount about a fish
which is not subject to our control and the conditions of whose life we are not able to reproduce
satisfactorily for purposes of experiment. At least
so it humbly seems to me.

Other than ordinary observation and such simple
experiment as rearing fry and parr from the egg
stage, the means employed in developing our
knowledge have been marking the fish and studying
the structure of their scales.

Small salmon when in the smolt stage on their
first descent to the sea have been marked with a
loop of silver wire in the back fin and have been
recaptured on their return as adult fish. Larger
salmon, both kelt and clean, and in salt as well as
in fresh water, have been marked with a numbered
silver plate fastened to the base of the dorsal fin
by means of wires passing through the fin. On
recapture not only may part of their journey be
traced in many cases but also the rate and amount
of growth during their absence is known since
particulars of length and weight are, or should be,
recorded on both occasions.

A most surprising fact is that not only the exact
age but also the complete history and growth
throughout life can be read from the scales of every

salmon. The process, which in recent years has
been developed into an exact science, had its origin
a couple of hundred years ago, but only in the
early years of this century was it applied with any
precision and then first of all to cod scales. The
late Mr. H. W. Johnston among others took up
the study of the subject as applied to salmon two
or three years after the first work on cod, and since
then it has been extended not only for the original
fish and that with which we are now dealing but
also for most of the other important marine and
freshwater fishes.

The theory on which the reading of scales is based
can be stated very shortly. A fish acquires a complete coating of scales very early in life and from
then onwards the increasing area of the body surface
continues to be covered, not by an increase in the
number of scales, but by an increase in the size of
each scale which was originally laid down. The
growth, moreover, on the more deeply bedded part
of the scale (the visible portion is only about one
third of the whole) takes the form of an orderly
array of ridges. These, viewed through the micro-
scope by transmitted light, have the appearance of
lines, one series being bold and widely spaced and
the next and narrower band finer and closer together.
In an adult salmon scale there is also a fine and rather
small central portion and a coarser and larger outer
section. The widely spaced ridges represent the
growth of a summer, the narrow band that of a
winter. The small central portion registers the
river, and the larger, coarser outer part the sea, life.
Scale growth is not only differentiated and zonal
but is also proportional to the growth of the body
so that the length of the fish at any time of its life
can be calculated from appropriate measurements
of the scales.

So much for the methods, the results are perhaps
of more interest.

Clean salmon may ascend our larger rivers on

almost any day of the year when the water is suitable
provided man has not entirely upset the works of
Nature. But they normally spawn only between the
middle of October and the end of February and the
majority in either November or December.

Some therefore have a very long wait in fresh
water. It is possibly twelve months before they
spawn and several months thereafter before they
regain the sea. During this period they do not
feed but exist on the fat and other materials brought
in with them from the sea. Very occasionally a
fish may be found which has consumed a meal ;
one fish in December in the Tweed which had taken
some parr, two or three kelts in Ireland which had
swallowed May flies, and so on, but they only form
the rare exceptions which prove the rule. The
salmon consequently when in fresh water become
steadily thinner and at the same time they lose
their silveriness ; the males become red, blotched
with black and dirty yellow, and at the same time
an enormous snout is produced by the extension of
both jaws, the development of a large hook on
the lower and a receptive cavity for it at the end of
the upper. The females are less highly coloured,
are rather black and dingy, and have no development of the jaws. At this stage the male is often
referred to as a kipper.

What may be the use of the male hooked jaw is
not known. The most usual explanation is that
it is merely a secondary sexual character. It is
certainly not used in the construction of the redd or
mound in which the eggs are deposited. The male
takes no active part in the preparation of this nursery.

For spawning the fish select if possible a place
where the water runs fairly rapidly and the bottom
consists of gravel of the size of one's fist downwards.
They are also very fond of the tail of a pool just
where the glide develops into the more rapid stream
down below. The female is the worker. The male
beats off other males which would usurp his place

and trout which endeavour to devour the eggs. The males also make a nuisance of themselves generally within the areas which they regard as their own. Occasionally two males will fight a battle, and I once saw two alternately chase and fight each other for two hundred yards or so up a rapid shallow stream until both were completely exhausted. Usually, however, the smaller considers discretion the better part of valour and beats a hasty retreat.

In making the redd the female turns on her side and with a sharp fanning motion of her tail moves some of the gravel downstream. During this process no eggs are shed but from time to time the female remains quiescent and the male moves up alongside her. A ' pocket ' of eggs is then extruded and, practically simultaneously, the male sheds a small ' cloud ' of milt to fertilize them. The female then resumes the fanning motion and rapidly covers with gravel the pocket of eggs. Ultimately the female's exertions form a mound composed of a mixture of stones and salmon eggs.

When she has finished spawning the female drops downstream to the nearest pool or if she be in the tail water of a pool she may move up into the deeper water above. The male, however, may remain in or about the newly made hole for two or three days or he may go off with another female. The proportion of males is high among grilse and almost all the very large fish are also of this sex, but in the whole salmon population two females usually exist for every male so that polygamy is normal and a necessity.

A redd is easily distinguished at the spawning season since the gravel is then obviously freshly moved. If in a firm terrain and not much disturbed by floods it may even be still more or less in shape in the following summer. A characteristic is that often a few stones too large to move by tail and current alone remain at the bottom of the hole and this differentiates it from the somewhat similar shapes sometimes carved by the unaided stream in

rather soft and deep gravel. The amount of
material which may be moved by a fish of even
moderate size is surprising. A female of twenty
pounds or so will usually create a mound containing
several barrow-loads of stones.

The time required for the development of the
eggs to the hatching stage is directly dependent
upon the water temperature. When the water is
warm the time is shorter than when it is cold. At
43° F. the period is approximately ninety days,
but when about 50° as little as seventy days may
suffice. When only 33° to 35° from 150 to 160 days
may be necessary.

When hatched the little fish, then known as
alevins, are as unlike salmon as it is possible to be.
Weighed down by a yolk sac larger than their own
bodies, on the contents of which they exist wholly
for a month and partly for another fortnight or so,
they lie in the gravel and indeed have little power
of free movement, although if disturbed they
instinctively seek a dark corner as if for protection.
With the yolk sac partially gone and consequently
more able to swim and keep on an even keel they
begin to emerge from the stones and to supplement
their self-contained ration with external food.

This commencement of feeding after about four
weeks and before the yolk sac is completely absorbed
is an important fact to be borne in mind when fry
from a hatchery are about to be liberated. They
should be released at the time when natural feeding
would commence and not only after the yolk sac
has completely disappeared.

It is undoubtedly at this stage that one of the
highest rates of mortality throughout the life of
the salmon occurs. Various factors may contribute
to the absence or paucity of food and to the inability
or unwillingness of the fish to absorb it. Undoubtedly many enemies also then take a heavy
toll. Birds and fish alike descend on them. Ducks,
mergansers, goosanders, water rails, probably also

herons, coots, and water hens, come from above ; brown trout, eels, parr, miller's thumbs, and so on are in the water. Of the list it is difficult to pick the worst.

Those of the alevins which survive develop into fry as soon as the yolk sac has entirely disappeared and these in turn become parr in their first summer.

Parr are very like trout in appearance and often the question is asked as to how the two species may be distinguished. For the angler who is not a scientist and has not the scientific equipment two main points of differentiation exist. In the salmon the maxillary bone, the little pear-shaped bone at each side of the mouth, extends only as far as immediately below the centre of the eye ; in the trout its hinder edge is below or beyond the posterior edge of the eye. An even more easily distinguished feature is that the adipose fin (the little rayless fin on the hinder part of the back) is a semi-transparent slate, or of only the very palest yellow, colour in the salmon ; it is always a bright deep yellow or orange in the trout. The paired fins of the trout are also deeper in colour than the corresponding fins of the salmon. A distinction in the number of scales between the adipose fin and the lateral line counted from the front edge of the fin in a backward sloping row is of more service in helping to decide whether an adult fish is a salmon or sea trout. In the bigger species the number of scales is from ten to thirteen, usually eleven, and in the trout from thirteen to sixteen, usually fourteen.

In the extreme south of England a large proportion of the parr change into smolts and go to sea at the end of the first year of life, *i.e.* in April, May, or June of the year following that of hatching. But over the greater part of Great Britain and Ireland the vast majority of smolts are two years old. In the north of Scotland as much as a third of the total may remain in fresh water for a third year. The general rule not only here but in Norway,

the Baltic countries, and Eastern Canada is that the
more northerly the river the greater is the average
age of the smolts.

Parr resemble very strongly trout of similar size
though the so-called parr marks, vertical dark
marks along the sides which look as if they might
have been made by a smear from the tips of the
fingers, are more strongly developed in the parr.
Smolts on the other hand are bright, silvery little
creatures with the blue back and lighter underparts
of the adult fish. The change takes place in the
final two or three months of river life and is not
brought about by any new coat of scales or anything
of that sort. It is a purely surface change caused
by a deposit of a material known as guanin in the
skin. This guanin is in the form of light reflecting
plates and hence the silvery sheen, but if it be
removed by scraping the original parr markings will
be found still to exist in the deeper skin.

Once the smolts go to sea all track of them is
lost. They hang about near the top of the tideway
for a time then suddenly descend right out to salt
water on the ebb tide and commence that adventur-
ous journey from which apparently no more than
five per cent or so return.

Although we do not know where or how far they
go yet we do know without doubt, thanks to the story
of the scales, the period during which they are absent.

The earliest return as grilse in from twelve to
sixteen months after they left the river. Growth
has been rapid and a smolt of an ounce or two may
weigh from four to five pounds twelve months
later. The increase made is greatest during the
summer months, particularly at the end of July and
early in August, and the later grilse make a corresponding addition to their weight. In August
eight or nine pounds is a common size and grilse
of ten or twelve pounds are by no means great
rarities. The largest recorded is fourteen pounds.

It used to be thought that all salmon returned

first as grilse and then annually thereafter but we now know, again thanks to scale reading, this to be a fallacy. Only a proportion return as grilse and the remainder continue to feed and grow in the sea.

Some come back as small spring fish usually from eight to fifteen pounds in weight in the winter and spring after the grilse came in (*i.e.* when they have been rather less than two years in salt water). Others, weighing normally from fifteen to twenty-five pounds, come back in the summer of that same year, twelve months later than the grilse, and are called small summer salmon. Large springers and large summer fish are twelve months older, and ten pounds heavier, than the last two classes respectively and they nearly exhaust the original stock of smolts which went down to the sea in any one year. A very few fish may occasionally stay four or even five years in the sea without spawning and without coming to fresh water, but they are the exceptional fish of forty or more pounds of which we see so little and hear so much when they are captured.

The stock of fish therefore in a river is not entirely dependent upon the smolts of any one year but upon the migration of two or three years. In this is to be found a safeguard against the effects of an unusually small smolt run or an unusual mortality to a particular run in river or sea.

Practically all male salmon die after spawning, and although a very considerable proportion of the females which evade capture and live to spawn survive to reach the sea as kelts comparatively few, not more than ten per cent unless in very exceptional cases, come back again as clean fish.

The stock is composed therefore almost entirely of maiden salmon, and if we take the season as a whole not more than from two to five per cent of the total in the larger rivers are on their second return. In some of the smaller rivers the proportion may be rather higher, but everywhere a salmon which comes back for a third time is an exceptionally lucky fish and those on their fourth return are limited in the extreme.

We can be absolutely certain of these facts because during its adult freshwater life a salmon exists not only on its store of fat but also to a smaller extent upon the material of which the scales are composed. The absorption of the scale takes place from the edge inwards and in the kelt results in a partially ' worn ' scale with a ragged edge. On the resumption of growth and the deposition of new scale material a scar is formed at the junction of new and old which tells for all future time, so long as that fish or its scales exist, the story of the previous freshwater journey.

It will now be understood that some salmon are large not because of repeated spawning journeys but because they have devoted their time to constant feeding and growth. They are therefore not only ' maiden ' (which term is applied to both sexes and indicates being unspawned) but also relatively young. In fact the time consumed on a spawning journey, which may amount in the case of early spring (really winter) fish to as much as fifteen or seventeen months, is more than time lost as the fish is both fasting and actually losing, instead of gaining, weight. Condition begins to be lost from the day the fish stops feeding in the sea and continues until the day it regains salt water and again commences to take food. In the interval about one-third of its original gross weight will disappear.

When kelts return again to the river as clean fish they differ slightly in outward appearance from the maiden fish especially if they come back in the same year as that in which they went down. Kelts differ in this last respect. Some come back after only a few months and others after a full year in the sea. The former have usually been summer fish or grilse and the latter spring fish on their first visit to the river.

On the second return the spots on the gill covers are larger and rather more numerous than in the maiden fish and an additional number of spots will also be found scattered along the sides both above and below the lateral line. The fish generally have a more rough looking appearance on the surface of the skin than a maiden fish and the lower jaw has a very slight hook which causes many to be called males although almost all are of the opposite sex. If the gill covers be opened they will be found to be more or less infested with so-called ' gill maggots '—*lernæopoda salmonea*—the crustacean para-site which clean fish quickly acquire in fresh water and which kelts have in added numbers. These creatures can breed only in fresh water but can survive in salt water although they gradually die off there. For this last reason previously spawned fish which have been a year in the sea carry fewer of them than those which have been away only a few months, although in both cases damaged gill filaments from which the parasites have disappeared can be seen.

The fish on their second or subsequent return are sufficiently marked from the others to have given rise to doubts as to their identity and to be christened with a variety of names. The old theory was that they were either trout or a cross between salmon and trout and their most common appellation, still in extensive use, is ' bull trout.' In a part of Scotland they are also called Norwegian salmon or lax because, I presume, anything foreign must be inferior and the flesh of these fish is very much more pale than that of maiden salmon although both are equally rich in fat. Another local name is ' trouty salmon.'

The story of the salmon might be continued at some considerable length. Their journeys and their behaviour in progressing along the coast might be traced and the reasons for the variation in habit of spring, summer, and autumn fish might be argued. Sufficient, however, has probably been said to give a general outline of the life of the fish and for further details the reader must be referred to the more technical publications.

BIBLIOGRAPHY

ALFIERI, B. and MENZIES, W. J. M. *Where to Catch Salmon and Trout.* Country Life, 1937.

CALDERWOOD, W. L. *Salmon Rivers and Lochs of Scotland*, 2nd Edition. Arnold, 1921.

——*Salmon and Sea Trout.* Arnold, 1930.

CHAYTOR, A. H. *Letters to a Salmon Fisher's Sons.* 2nd Edition. John Murray, 1919.

GRIMBLE, AUGUSTUS. *Salmon and Sea Trout Rivers of England and Wales.* Kegan Paul, Trench, Trubner & Co., 1904.

——*Salmon Rivers of Ireland.* Kegan Paul, Trench, Trubner & Co., 1903.

HUTTON, J. ARTHUR. " Rod Fishing for Salmon in the Wye." *Fishing Gazette*, 1930.

——*The Life History of the Salmon.* Aberdeen University Press, 1924.

——Numerous papers in the *Salmon and Trout Magazine* from 1908 onwards.

MENZIES, W. J. M. *The Salmon : Its Life Story.* 2nd Edition. Blackwood, 1931.

——*Salmon Passes.* H.M. Stationery Office, 1934.

MOORE, HUBERT STUART. *Salmon and Fresh Water Fisheries Act*, 1923. Sweet & Maxwell, 1924.

NALL, G. H. *The Life of the Sea Trout.* Seeley Service, 1930.

PHAIR, CHARLES. *Atlantic Salmon Fishing.* New York.

PRYCE-TANNATT, T. E. *How to Dress Salmon Flies.* Black, 1914.

Salmon and Trout Magazine. Fishmongers' Hall. Quarterly since 1908.

STEWART, CHARLES. *The Law of Scotland relating to Rights of Fishing.* 2nd Edition. Clark, 1892.

TAVERNER, ERIC. *Salmon Fishing.* Lonsdale Library. Seeley Service, 1931.

WANLESS, H. *The Angler and the Thread Line.* Herbert Jenkins, 1932.

INDEX